LAW STUDENT REVIEWS

TRIAL &

M000036452

• "The book is ar turner... The bool lawyer and the effec.... and emotionally.... It was a great eye-opener into the complicated world of criminal law....I can't wait for a sequel!"

• "TRIAL & ERROR has re-ignited my passion for law.... Every story taught me something about criminal law. I would recommend this book to anyone considering or enrolled in law school. The book is an exceptional account of the battles won and lost in the world of freedom lawyering and the pursuit of justice."

• "TRIAL & ERROR is very insightful not only to criminal law but to the world of legal practice and life. Each case captured an important lesson of being an attorney.... The book is an interesting, honest insight into the criminal law that I've never experienced before.... It has given me a much more realistic idea of what the field of criminal law is out in the real world.

• "The book provides comical relief and hope for someone with the aspiration of one day achieving success as a trial lawyer.... From the moment I picked up this book I was immediately rejuvenated."

• "TRIAL & ERROR has shown me that rapport with clients and people in general makes an outstanding lawyer.... It also highlights mistakes made by the budding defense attorney and what was learned from them.... I too struggle with public speaking and eloquence. Reading of the author's struggle inspired me....The cases exemplify what is essential to becoming a successful trial lawyer."

• "After reading TRIAL & ERROR my perspective on defense attorneys has completely changed....The book is truly inspiring.... The entire book was a learning experience....The cases all seemed to cover different moral dilemmas.... I am more inclined to become an attorney, so that I can fight injustices such as these."

• "Reading TRIAL & ERROR made me realize that the law is not as black and white as it may seem in our casebooks; it's far from that. There are shadows and doubts on both sides of every case.... It discloses the progression all lawyers must make from their days of law school idealism to the realities of legal practice.... This book taught me that a freedom lawyer's job is the hardest and highest calling."

• "TRIAL & ERROR ignites flames inside the belly of its readers. It places them side by side with a warrior of justice, page-by-page, case-by-case....There is always room for improvement if you stand outside the 'box' and evaluate yourself as a professional. This is the most important thing I took away from Arthur Campbell's experience as a criminal defense attorney....I find myself more interested than ever in this field of law."

• "This book inspires and serves as a reality check.... It opened my eyes to situations I had not yet considered, and to the disheartening moments of frustration the eager 1L forgets to prepare for.... It would have been helpful to read this book in the beginning of the semester as an introduction to criminal law."

• "I believe that every first-year law student should read this book. It helped me understand facets of criminal law that I most likely would not learn through textbooks and is definitely a must-read."

• TRIAL & ERROR reveals "the lawyer's struggle between the idealistic balancing of the scales of justice with the reality of the justice system.... I feel a bit more prepared for those moments that I am sure I will have for the rest of my life, where I will question the justice of the law I devote my days to....The book was a very encouraging read because it shows that it won't be easy, but if you work hard it will be worth it."

TRIAL & ERROR
The Education of a Freedom Lawyer
Volume One: For the Defense
Arthur W. Campbell

TRIAL & ERROR

TRIAL & ERROR

The Education
of a
Freedom Lawyer

Volume Two:
For the Prosecution

by
Arthur W. Campbell

Poetic Matrix Press

The average case, the case for which all the legal forms and rules are devised... does not exist at all, because every case, every crime... as soon as it really occurs, at once becomes a quite special case, and sometimes it is absolutely unlike anything that has ever happened before.

—Fedor Dostoevsky

The "whole truth" on which the court insists, is menacingly unfathomable: the whole truth is neither false nor true but is false and true.

—Tom Larson

The principal task of lawyers is remembering. We are to remember past events so that we may learn from them.

—Mike Tigar

CONTENT

Dedicated to all freedom lawyers
past, present, and future
who did or will train under
the E. Barrett Prettyman program
at Georgetown University Law School.

And to Stephanie Sanchez
of California Western School of Law,
secretary extraordinaire.

FOREWORD

by Jerry Coughlan, Coughlan Semmer & Lipman,
Former Assistant U.S. Attorney in Washington, D.C. and San Diego

In this second of his three-book series, Art Campbell
colorfully describes courtrooms well known to lawyers
who toil in the trenches of criminal law. I know. I was Art's
colleague as an Assistant U.S. Attorney in Washington, D.C. and
had very similar experiences. Like Art, I spent several months
in the misdemeanor trial courts at the start of my (what
turned out to be) ten-year career as a prosecutor. Like Art, I
lost my first two misdemeanor trials, and determined to learn
from my mistakes. And like Art, I had to deal with convicting
a man who I believed was innocent. This book reminded me,
and will educate all readers, of the often bizarre but
incredibly important role our criminal justice system plays in
our country, despite its many imperfections.

From what at first may seem ordinary misdemeanor
cases, Campbell unearths latent drama. He writes about the
colorful and diverse ways defendants, witnesses and jurors
act in a courtroom. He discloses "testilying" witnesses and his
struggles to skewer them on cross-examination. He exposes
strong-willed judges, determined to rule their courts at all
costs. Art reveals how seemingly routine cases hide surprises
that jurors may see but lawyers sometimes miss.

For a period of time our office assigned Art to try
cases before the most eccentric, irascible anti-prosecution
judge in the courthouse. Art's battles with Horace L. Bachover
(with whom I also enjoyed more than one go-around) range
from seriously constitutional ("A Jury of One's Peers") to
ludicrously carnal ("Heads Up, Officer").

Reading these accounts puts you in *real* courtrooms,
real trials, and the mind of a *real* prosecutor, not some
fictitious media portrayal. I hope you enjoy this book as
much as I did.

INTRODUCTION

Who are freedom lawyers? They come in all sizes, ages, genders, and eras. They carry an array of interests and skills. They labor in every area of society all over the globe. What they share is a determination to oppose injustice in whatever form it appears.

I began as a criminal defense lawyer. My first two years of courtroom battles are portrayed in Volume I of this series.

At that time I thought only defense attorneys could practice freedom law in criminal courts. Only they could fight unwarranted arrests, unreasonable searches, coerced confessions, vindictive prosecutions, unfair trials, and irrational sentences.

I might have clung to such one-sided views had I not been granted an E. Barrett Prettyman Fellowship at Georgetown Law. This master's program let me move across the aisle and become a Special Assistant United States Attorney in Washington, D.C.

When I joined the prosecution team I knew I'd have to shoulder an extra ethical burden. On defense my only obligation was to fight fairly for each client's rights. As prosecutor I'd have two responsibilities: to convict the guilty and to render justice.

This volume tracks my attempts to satisfy both demands. It also reveals an inner battle I discovered as a prosecutor: My vow to practice freedom law often struggled with my warrior's will to win.

So two issues surge beneath all these accounts: *Can I practice freedom law as a prosecutor? Can I fight to win and still fight fair?* Only after the last trial in this book did I find satisfactory answers. The discovery redirected my career.

As in volume one, the names of most participants are fictionalized, protecting both innocent and guilty, truth-tellers and liars, victims and scoundrels.

Each episode portrays a trial or hearing in the sequence it occurred; in between I've skipped a few to keep this volume manageable.

These trials were not celebrated; only some found mention on back pages of the WASHINGTON POST. But each had life-altering impacts on defendants, victims, witnesses, friends, and families

Indeed, the heart of justice beats inside low-profile trials like these, where each day citizens must face the awesome power of their government. For them our Constitution and the adversary system suddenly become much more than civics lessons and abstract ideals. If such cases fail to render justice, democracy will wither at its roots.

These trials also demonstrate another truth. Countless human dramas, each taut with surprise and someone's failure to communicate, unfold in our courtrooms every day. They mark our current place in history's march as law attempts to civilize the human clan.

* * * * *

The Education
of a
Freedom Lawyer

FIRST DAY "DOING JUSTICE"

A cold November dawned when I climbed in our rusted-out Camaro, christened "Yellow Bird" in early married years. It first had flown on California freeways, then strained up icy mountain roads to law school.

I flashbacked to one night the Bird was clutched by swirling waters of a hurricane; three beefy volunteers pushed it free before my wife and I were swept away. Today the Bird—still redolent of soaked interior—would churn through rush-hour traffic surging toward the District of Columbia.

This morning I would trade my hard-won title of defense attorney for another ponderous name: Special Assistant United States Attorney for Washington, D.C. My desk would rest within a suite of rooms inside Superior Court.

As a lawyer for defendants, trudging up the courthouse steps, I used to ask myself, *When prosecutor offices cuddle next to those of judges, do they erode a bedrock principle of our government, the separation of powers?*

A client once insisted that each evening judges in some hidden room clinked glasses with prosecutors, toasting one more day of rounding up the city's indigents and tossing them in jail.

With anticipation riddled by uncertainty, I backed the Yellow Bird out of our gravel driveway in Virginia's countryside. Soon I was heading down a thirty-mile stretch of parkway named for our first president.

Exiting the parkway under corrugated clouds, I braked at a stoplight, revving the Camaro's engine to avoid a stall.

* * * * *

Judges I'd appeared before marched across my mind. Most had risen from the ranks of prosecutors, touting "tough-on-crime." That trait seemed essential for appointment or election to the bench.

I'd watched furrows deepen in these jurists' brows from parades of citizens, ninety percent of whom were bowed beneath plea-bargains where they had to cop to some kind of crime. Was it any wonder that these judges acted from a gut belief in most defendants' guilt?

Did Dame Justice don her blindfold so she wouldn't see her scales droop when judges leaned unconsciously upon the prosecutor's side? Adding my weight to this tray, how could I maintain the pledge I made before I entered law school, that I'd only use my skills to practice freedom law?

For weeks my mind had sought for ways to handle these disturbing doubts. Sometimes it fastened on a fact most citizens don't know, one seldom headlined in mass media: Prosecutors actually are charged to serve two masters: their "client" and "the cause of justice."

In prior days as counsel for defense my single obligation was to serve my client ethically. Now I'd get to toughen litigation muscles, hefting double duties as a prosecutor.

I'd seen many prosecutors, glowing from the heat of trial or spotlights of the press, forget their second pledge or blindly blend the two. My hope was to seize the prosecutor's duty to do justice as my way to practice freedom law.

But would my office let me offer counter-weights when Blindfold Belle held up unbalanced scales? Could I include the larger costs to our community when I decided whom to charge with what? In short, could I align the goals of freedom law with those of the government? How ironic that these aims were often posed as separate!

* * * * *

As the traffic signal switched from red to green, I snapped from my reverie and let out the clutch. Soon I joined a

4

swarm of Washingtonians cruising for rare parking spots like hornets searching for a peach.

Eventually I nosed the Bird into a place beside a junkyard with a Doberman who barked, "Hey-hey-hey!" I thumbed a dozen quarters in a death's-head meter; that would save me from a tow-truck until noon.

Swinging strangely empty hands—as yet I had no case to brief—I climbed the courthouse stairs and strode along a marble-tiled hall. I pushed against the brass plate on a hefty door whose black-etched lettering proclaimed, "United States Attorney's Office."

As the door hissed shut behind me, I tried to cloak my nervousness inside a look of confident humility and headed for a trim receptionist ensconced behind a steel desk.

"Hi, I'm Art Campbell, the new guy on your team." Not shattered by my charm, she flashed a cordial smile and asked for my credentials. I reached inside the jacket of my dark-blue suit and, self-consciously enacting what I'd seen on films and television, flipped the flap of my new leather folder.

God, what a power symbol! One side trumpeted "United States Department of Justice" from an embossed seal. Gleaming from the other side was my laminated face. I imagined flashing it at crime scenes as I pushed through mobs of cops, reporters, gawkers" *How cool would that be?*

The receptionist rose smoothly from her chair. "Please follow me, Mr. Campbell. My name's Roberta Closon, but Bobbi works just fine."

She led me down a row of plexiglass-walled cubicles where I glimpsed lawyers bent in frozen postures over legal pads and files—until they spotted me. *Who let that defense attorney in?!*

Closon stopped outside an open doorway to the largest office. Clovis Bankwood looked up, dropped a file folder he'd been holding, and hauled his six-foot bulk out of a leather swivel chair. "Hi, Art!"

At thirty-eight, Bankwood was chief U.S. prosecutor for D.C. Superior Court. "Let me take you to your temporary office." *Was there a veiled warning in those words?*

He showed me a ten-by-ten-foot room with walls of bureaucratic beige; coffee stains had mapped out kingdoms on a once-green carpet. As I eased into the creaky wooden chair behind an oaken desk, I faced two armless metal seats, the only other furniture. One window waiting for a wash stared out at the street.

Two thick paper-back editions of D.C. and U.S. codes leaned against each other on the desk. Next to them a telephone held down a sheaf of crime-charging sheets: court's copy white, defense counsel's pink, prosecutor's yellow. On the floor a cardboard box held stacks of empty file jackets and a menagerie of poke-and-bend-back clips.

"We'll start you in papering before we turn you loose inside a courtroom. Listen hard to the arresting cops who bring you cases," Clovis warned, "but only charge what we can prove beyond a reasonable doubt. Your trial experience should help you here. Check with me if you're unsure what crime to bring or drop—or if somebody questions your authority. And...oh, welcome aboard!"

Bankwood flashed a politician's smile, pivoted, and strode down the hall.

* * * * *

Papering. Prosecutors have enormous power to charge others with a crime. Most people only see this process through the smoky lens of mainstream media.

T.V shows jump-start episodes with slam-bam scenes of criminal activity, stoking viewers' zeal to see the perp get caught. Eventually the suspect's tossed into a drama-laden trial.

6

Since audiences have seen the crime, a law of human nature—more brawny than the nymph of "presumed innocence"—spurs their passion as the plot unfolds: *Lock away that criminal—don't let some crafty lawyer cover up his guilt with constitutional concerns or pry him off the hook with reasonable doubt about the evidence!*

In real life less than ten percent of those arrested go to trial. The rest throw away presumptions of their innocence and other constitutional rights. The latters' forfeitures take place at high-stakes gambling sessions, a.k.a. "negotiated pleas."

Who selects the cards to deal at plea-bargain tables and which to turn face-up at trial? Who decides if there will be a game at all?

This life-changing power rests with prosecutors who "paper" cases. They choose what crimes have been committed and—supposedly—if prosecuting them will serve the ends of justice.

In D.C. this crucial job was done by squads of young attorneys fresh from law school, most with zero hours in a courtroom. Yet, nudged by savvy and ambitious cops, new recruits were tasked to charge what they thought could be proved at trial.

When papering a case we penned the names of officers and witnesses on the outside of a file-folder. On inside flaps we summarized the evidence at hand to prove each element of crime we charged. We stapled in related papers: arrest reports, rap sheets, lab tests, photos, etc.

Papering a misdemeanor (crimes worth a year or less in jail) took about one-half an hour. After the defendant was arraigned in court, that file slept with others in a box until its day of trial.

An effective paperer would need to know both the U.S. and D.C. Codes of crime, rules of evidence, office policies, plus propensities of local jurors.

As I already knew the law and courtroom rules, a senior colleague sat me down and briefed me on our policies, e.g., zero-tolerance for illegal weapons. I *thought* I knew how D.C. juries viewed the world, but in this realm I had much more to learn.

* * * * *

Papering my first four cases took me less than ninety minutes. In my office cops crouched on those armless chairs, reciting facts and handing over documents.

Each crime I selected seemed to pop from first-year law exams: assault (technically a "battery"), two shopliftings ("petty larcenies" in legalese), and "sol pros" (soliciting an "undercover" cop for prostitution.)

I'd encountered these offenses as counsel for defense. With skepticism honed from handling charges from the other side, I probed beneath each search and seizure, each arrest and questioning of suspects.

I was pleasantly surprised I couldn't scent a whiff of violated rights. All facts had been eye-balled by police or witnesses they'd interviewed. Freedom lawyer didn't feel the slightest kick against his shins.

Then a grizzled plainclothes officer paused outside my door. Wearing drab slacks and a short-sleeved shirt, he'd hooked his sport coat by a thumb and slung it on one shoulder. His other hand clutched papers rolled into a scroll.

Without a word he moseyed in, unrolled his papyrus upon my desk, and dropped his big-boned body on a metal chair. From his report I saw his name was "Sergeant Barstow Jenkins."

Instead of chatting up his case, he sat in silence waiting for some word from me. But my proclivity to break the ice was squelched by my resistance to his blatant alpha gambit in "my" office.

I slowly thumbed through his report. Last night he'd stopped a car, found a thirty-eight tucked in the wheel-well inside its trunk, and charged the driver with C.P.W.L. (Carrying a Pistol Without a License.)

How did all this start? Where's the legal cause for Jenkins' stop? His report just said he'd seen a cruising car that "looked suspicious" and sped away when the sergeant's black-and-white approached. To me it was the bust itself that looked suspicious.

All right, Sarge, I'll yield round one in this macho contest: I'll speak first.

"So, Jenkins, how did you figure this guy had a gun? Did you get a roll-call flyer, witness tip, or radio-run describing the driver or his car? Watch him case some target? Spot a broken taillight?"

"Nah," the sergeant scoffed, "it just didn't feel right to see a black kid cruising through an all-white neighborhood at three a.m.—then take off when he spotted me."

He drew up his torso, proud as a prince's cat: "Call it 'law-enforcement instinct.' And see? Clearly I was right. Found a gun inside his trunk. Zero tolerance—that's your policy on guns."

"But sergeant, I can't justify your search and seizure without legal cause. You didn't have a legit reason for your stop. Even law-and-order judges would exclude the gun as seized unconstitutionally."

Jenkins stared at me as if my skin had broken out in lawfulness. "Just file the charge, assistant," he growled. "This guy's got another pending charge," receiving stolen property. Odds are he'll cop a plea to this if someone drops the R.S.P." He held my gaze with rapt vacuity.

I felt adrenalin surge into my chest. This was the kind of cop I'd gone to law school to combat: a law-enforcement missile without stabilizing fins.

I dialed down my anger, hoping that he wouldn't take my lowered voice for weakness. "Sorry, Jenkins, I won't file what I can't prove in court with valid evidence."

Is this my test for loyalty to "law and order," the kind conveniently ignoring that our Bill of Rights is part of "law?" Has someone directed Jenkins to the virginal D.A., that former counsel for defense, to see if I can view the world through prosecutor's eyes? Should I leave the room, consult my boss, get his authority to "no-paper" this improper bust?

No! Bankwood said to check with him if I became uncertain—and I'm dead sure about this case. If Jenkins wants to stir up trouble, bring it on.

I held his gaze to see which way he'd move: capitulate or escalate.

"Okay," he sighed and heaved his body from the chair. Then Jenkins caught me by surprise. He smiled, reached across the desk, and shook my hand.

"I know you had to do what you just did." He winked and added, "But at least that's one more gun that won't be shooting me." He gathered up his documents and ambled down the hall.

I could hardly wait til lunch to shut my office door and grab the phone. On the second ring my wife picked up. I described the episode with Jenkins; my first go at freedom-law as a prosecutor.

"You won't believe this, Dru, but I just did more justice in ten minutes as a prosecutor than I could have done in weeks for the defense!"

* * * * *

The next few days in papering I was glad to see how rarely even newbie colleagues papered cases in a rash of prosecutor fever. Seldom did they get infected by cops' rabid exhortations, "Lock-'em-up!" regardless of the evidence, the Constitution, or net loss to society.

I did, however, catch a mild strain of office schizophrenia. It blew through our hallways half a dozen times each day from cops with marijuana busts. Pot triggered fierce bi-polar views inside our ranks, one end reeking with hypocrisy.

Some prosecutors toked a spliff at night, then came to work next day and sent folks to the jug for doing the same thing.

At the other pole sat true-believer colleagues plying their own moral codes. They regarded Texas tea as harmless to democracy. So they reached out for reefer busts and scratched "*NO PAPER*" over every less-than-two-joint case they found. (Apparently their private codes were bound with quantitative threads.)

I staked a wobbly claim between these two extremes. I told pot-pinching cops who came to me to keep walking down the hall and find another paperer. Although I thought weed should be legalized, I refused to carve exceptions in the law with my own pocket knife.

* * * * *

By Friday evening I had served five days in papering. I drove home in Yellow Bird, pondering my first week as prosecutor.

I'd begun with qualms that I could use my skills to throw a fellow citizen in jail. But this week I'd found the power to ensure—at least in cases I would handle—constitutional rights would triumph over bogus busts.

When I scrawled "*NO PAPER*" on illicit searches, sham confessions, or improper evidence, I served the Blindfold Lady long before defendants looked to her in court.

But as my Camaro's tires scrunched the gravel on our rural driveway, I heard whispers from our fallow carrot patch: *This week you only worked behind a desk. Can you try a case in court and practice freedom law?*

11

WELCOME TO MISDEMEANOR TRIALS

*Experience is what you get when you don't get
what you want.* —Randy Pausch

Gods of scarce resources issued a decree that our office couldn't staff its misdemeanor trials with veteran attorneys. Lawyers with experience must be saved for felonies. That meant only battle-seasoned felony attorneys had the luxury of hands-on trial preparation weeks before a judge's hammer dropped.

In D.C.'s misdemeanor world, prosecutors who had never stood in court initially decided what crimes could be proved by colleagues who'd just joined the litigation squad. Result? The least experienced handed half-inflated footballs to the least prepared.

On the day a misdemeanor would be tried, a judge gave me five to fifteen minutes to prepare the prosecution's case. The stopwatch clicked when the arresting officer entered court and plunked our case file in my hand.

Deciphering scribbles in this file, I raced to formulate a strategy, compose an opening statement, sort through potential witnesses, and choose lines of questioning. Next I scanned the courtroom, checked what witnesses had actually appeared and—if time permitted—asked them to step forward and confer.

I loved trying misdemeanors. I learned more moves and got more rushes of adrenalin than any other time in court.

But only as a prosecutor did I learn that I was steered by something other than my pledge to freedom law.

My freedom lawyer searched for larger equities inside each case and tried to see them actualized. Like an imagined charger from my childhood, years ago he guided me to law school's doors. Now he gladly bore my prosecutor's duty to "do justice" where I could.

But I also had a fighter side. A horse bred just for war, he transformed every trial into a contest I must win. I rationalized his presence as the power for my prosecutor's other duty, "serve your client well." He muscled past each obstacle until he reached the victor's circle where jurors shouted, *Guilty, Guilty, GUILTY!*

Sometimes when a verdict didn't go his way, fighter's blinkers blocked his eyes from seeing freedom lawyer's larger view: that the government *should* lose trials where defendants' peers are not convinced beyond a reasonable doubt. Those times, instead of bathing in adrenalin from a hard-fought bout, warrior brooded self-indulgently upon "his loss."

Usually both parts of my nature pulled together like a well matched team. Thus I could live out boyhood fantasies and feel like a "champion of justice." At those times my thoughts were mainly tactical: how best deploy my instinct for the kill so it secured a proper win.

But other times I felt tension spring between my fighter and my freedom lawyer. A minor instance happened every time I introduced myself in court. As a defense attorney I had chafed when prosecutors boasted they were lawyers for "the government," "the people," or "the United States."

Imagine being the accused when a bailiff booms out, "The United States of America versus You." The image triggers terror: a collective father-figure facing down some miscreant. It raises prehistoric hackles of the human pack, pitting the community against an individual.

Yet when I became a prosecutor, warrior seized the chance to introduce himself this way. He shushed freedom lawyer's whispers that appeals to a jury's primal urges clobbered rationality and crippled a defendant's right to parity before the bar.

Once, near the end of my encounters in this book, warrior grabbed the bit and galloped to the finish line. In the process it stampeded a defendant who was innocent into a cage with steel bars.

After the event I dug into my soul and faced why it occurred. But I still ponder that finalé, how it changed the course of my career, how in retrospect each case on these pages posted warning signs along the way.

* * * * *

My first trial for the government had a rousing title: "Assault with a Deadly Weapon," shorthanded "A.D.W. (Pipe)."

A supermarket manager had surprised a stranger in his storage room. The intruder rushed the manager, waved a two-foot pipe five inches from his face, then dashed outside. He threw his weapon in some weeds beside the door and ran into a cop.

What handicapped my case was zero presence of dramatic evidence. No one thought to grab the pipe and nobody got hurt. Still, warrior rode relentless through this empty valley, confident that he could easily prove the legal meaning of "assault." The D.C. Code asserted this meant *threatened* harmful or offensive contact. (Real contact was called "battery.")

Fighter brushed aside the power of common parlance to frame outcomes of a trial. But in the world at large "assaults" require contact. To D.C. jurors no harm meant no foul. "Not guilty" was their call.

Ironically my warrior even helped the jury reach their bottom line. The defendant took the stand and boldly claimed he'd never had a weapon in his hand. On cross-exam I hit him with three shots that should have blown apart his credibility. I got him to admit he'd been recently convicted of plain robbery, armed robbery, and assault.

But when I talked with jurors after trial, I learned this was overkill. It persuaded them that he'd been through enough. They gave my supermarket manager full marks for veracity, but mere assault was nothing matched against defendant's other crimes and sentences he'd face.

My second trial was another A.D.W. with morbid overtones: "Assaults with Lye and Knife." Once again the case was papered sans persuasive evidence: No prints on a merely brandished knife, no lye bottle, no lab tests, no scorched clothing, no photos of burned arms, no scars remaining by the time of trial.

Still, on the trial's second day, warrior—blinded by his will to win—felt he'd spanned this chasm of non-evidence with stout eye-witness testimony. Both male and female victims described in detail how defendant had attacked them in their home when she discovered she'd become one's jilted lover.

During his summation, counsel for defense unleashed a potent argument: "If the government's so sure that these assaults even occurred, why didn't Mr. Campbell show you fingerprints, a lye bottle, chemist's testimony, clothing, photos, scars..." etcetera.

As welcomed as a soup stain on my tie, I tried to downplay what I called this "desperate defense." I told jurors all they needed in this case was to believe our clearly truthful witnesses. "Surely you don't need to see all evidence that's *possible*, even the kitchen sink."

Twenty minutes after the presiding judge sent jurors to deliberate, they trooped back to let their foreman state, "Not guilty."

I felt like a boxer, confident until his losing score's announced, then suddenly aware his mind's not been following the real fight. Convinced of the defendant's guilt, I slumped in my chair until the final juror sauntered out.

So warrior lost his first two trials for the government. Always given to extremes, he pondered a remark from the once-vanquished Bonaparte: "Glory can be fleeting but obscurity's forever."

In a punky funk I shoved papers in my briefcase and trudged from court. Trying to salvage something useful from the wreck, my mind searched for lessons I could use another day.

Did warrior blind you to a D.C. jury's jaundiced views about the government? Did he mount his rhino of denial and charge past all those rocks of doubt?

Wait a minute! freedom lawyer shouted. *Don't these wimwams of defeat arise from overlooking how our system is supposed to work? Has fighter totally forgotten his allegiance to due process and his oath to freedom law?*

That question thrust a sword of irony into my gut.

Okay, I muttered to myself, *Defendants should be freed unless their guilt is clear beyond a reasonable doubt, and doubts piled up inside those two trials like dirty dishes in a basement flat.*

Yes, I still believe it's better that a dozen guilty folks go free than one blameless lout get tossed in Skookum House. But, damn it, warrior hates to lose!

Although overall I relished misdemeanor trials, those losses on my fighter's pleasure scale ranked right below two mangled thumbs.

When I reviewed these cases with my boss, I wondered if he'd step me back to papering. Bankwood only grinned. "Don't worry, Art. Trying misdemeanors are how prosecutors cut their teeth. You learn to think fast on your feet and fight with what you've got at hand. It's the fastest way to hone your trial skills."

As I exited my boss's office, warrior added his own pep talk: *You haven't lost your courtroom skills. You only overlooked the way a D.C. jury views the prosecution's case. Next time blow away your mental dust and see what's really going on.*

However, I'd not realized how much my former boxer's will to win could warp my estimate of what I faced inside the ring. Nor had I plumbed how it could sometimes numb my loyalty to freedom law.

So, walking to my office, I felt fighter throwing back his chest: *Next time I'll make my case so strong it parries every fist of doubt.*

BACKHANDED SWITCHBLADE

Failure is feedback.
—Billie Jean King

Today I vowed I wouldn't underestimate the clout of doubt
on jurors' minds nor overestimate the power of my case. I'd
use what I had learned; I didn't want to lose again.

Sitting next to me in court was colleague Mergot Dietz.
She'd graduated near the top of Indiana Law and joined our
office seven weeks ago.

Since she'd never tried a case, Mergot asked to second-chair,
see how things were done. My suspicious side imagined
Bankwood placed her here to check if I, prior die-hard
lawyer for defense, was trying hard enough to throw
defendants in the can.

Our judge, still waiting in his chambers, would be Oram
Klezky, notorious for short-fused detonations from the bench.
He often sat in court and glared at passing folk below the
window, hand upon his gavel, poised to bash the slightest
hint of villainy.

Despite his show-boat style, hardnosed Klezky was an even-
handed masher, hammering both lawyers for defendants and
the government.

In the gallery a dozen watchers slouched on pew-like
benches, hoping they could witness some of Klezky's
fireworks. No doubt they also wondered why our office
needed double lawyers in his court.

Like a scream in church, the telephone erupted on our court
clerk's desk; its ring had not been switched to light-bulb
mode. Mergot and I straightened in our chairs. The clerk
snatched the receiver, paused a moment, and announced, "A
trial's on its way, charge of P.P.W." (Possession of a Prohibited
Weapon.)

17

A minute later attorney Fred Wreight ambled through the door. He wore a saggy suit and twisted smile. He could be a litigation bulldog when his ego got aroused. But most days he was leashed to monetary gods so he could scarf up dough from court-appointment troughs. Fred Wreight hailed from Fifth Street.

Fifth Streeters, lawyers with a one-room office close to court, could harvest more dinero pleading five defendants guilty in an hour than taking time to try a case. They processed clients more than represented them. One scoffed, "Art, don't get so high and mighty. You and I are only courthouse janitors, brooming people back into the messes they've created for themselves."

When clients would insist on trial, Wreight could boogie with three forensic decades in his shoes. A better courtroom lawyer than his cronies, he brought cunning to the table for defense.

Wreight approached us, amping up his smile. "I've got a P.P.W.—switchblade. This gentleman," half-turning to a grim-faced man two strides behind, "is Mr. Darnan Burnell, the accused. Tell you what, Art. I'll go light on you today. We'll stipulate the knife your cop retrieved was found three feet from Mr. Burnell in a crowded bar."

Finally, concrete evidence! warrior whooped. Eager to secure this proof, I knew Wreight could be as tricky as a closet full of chimps. I answered, "Sounds okay to me, but wait until I see our jacket on the case."

"We'll also waive a jury," Wreight chirped, "and let Klezky try the charge." The clerk heard this, picked up the phone, and dialed the jurist's chambers.

"Fine with us," I said, remembering Mergot by my side. Klezky was a law-and-order judge, a former prosecutor whose first career of disbelieving all defendants had now ripened to a habit of juridical efficiency. He'd be inclined to see the facts our way. "What's in this for you?" I asked.

"Just want to save time for the government, the court, and...,"
Wreight winked, "...my other forty-dozen clients." Silently
my teeth ground at his motive although it seemed plausible.
Should I peer beneath it for some strategy?

A uniformed policeman quick-stepped through the door and
headed toward the prosecution desk. Looking at the file by
his thigh, I gathered he was the arresting officer. In his other
hand he clutched a brown lock-sealed envelope. I nudged
Mergot: "There's our knife, I hope."

Before the cop could reach our desk, the judge flung wide
his chamber door and, with a swirl of sable sleeves, entered
like a mob of bats. "Good morning!" Klezky sang out in a
high-pitched voice. He whisked away the bailiff's only
speech, delivering it himself: "Please be seated. Come to
order."

"Counsel for the government," he said focusing on me,
"you've got five minutes to decide which witness to call first."
He reached for his file of the case, spread it open on the
bench and, looking like a child with a birthday book, began
to read it to himself.

Our cop unfroze, pushed back the swinging wooden bar, and
proceeded to our desk. "I'm Bob Kienan, the arresting
officer." He bent down and handed Mergot our case file. She
opened it between us.

"Our only other witness," he continued in a whisper, "is a
waitress from the bar where the defendant had his knife." He
motioned for a woman in the gallery to join our group.

Karlotte Biagi, on the downhill side of thirty, propelled her
slinky body toward our desk, blonde curls jiggling in a fare-
thee-well. Nodding towards Burnell, she said, "I saw that guy
throw down a knife."

"That's fine," I said. "I'll call you after Officer Kienan testifies.
There won't be a jury. Just tell the judge exactly what you
saw." I stood up. "Your Honor, prosecution's ready."

Kienan told the court how he'd been dispatched to a bar on 13th Street. The bouncer pointed out a patron who, he said, had flashed a switchblade in the premises.

I paused for Wreight's objection based on hearsay grounds. It didn't come.

Q. Do you now see that patron in the courtroom?

A. Yes, sir. He's sitting right beside his counsel. He's defendant, Darnan Burnell.

The officer described how he had spun Burnell around, placed his suspect's palms upon the bar, and frisked him. When he couldn't find a knife, Kienan told Burnell and his two buddies it was closing time for them.

According to our officer, Burnell appeared agreeable and, after turning briefly to the bar, began moving toward the door. Then Kienan heard a female voice yell, "Look out" he's got it again!"

Warrior cheered: *Classic spontaneous utterance—an exception to the hearsay rule!* Wreight still failed to object.

Kienan told Burnell to freeze and saw him "backhand something from his grasp." The policeman scanned the floor and found a switchblade three feet from Burnell.

Q. When you retrieved it, was the blade exposed?

A. No sir, it was closed inside the clasp.

I knew it didn't matter that the knife was closed. Switchblades were *per se* illegal in D.C. Still, I didn't want defense to pluck this plum out of the evidence as if I'd tried to overcook my case.

Nodding to attorney Wreight, I announced our stipulation and introduced the knife from Kienan's envelope as government's Exhibit A. "Your witness," I declared and took my seat.

On cross-exam Wreight only asked one question: "Did I hear you correctly: You never said you *saw* my client hold that knife?"

"That's right," Kienan replied.

I glimpsed a shade of doubt slip through the courtroom window, fly toward Klezky's bench, and roost beside him like a hungry ghost. The jurist raised a pinky to explore his ear.

At least whoever papered charges for this switchblade-on-the-floor had subpoenaed one eyewitness to possession of the knife. I asked our waitress to come forward; she clacked her backless heels down the aisle to the witness chair.

Biagi reinforced Kienan's testimony. She was the one who'd screamed. What she'd seen defendant toss aside had been a folded knife.

"Your honor, may the record show the witness is referring to Exhibit A."

"Objection!" bellowed Wreight. "That's been only stipulated as the knife found on the *floor*."

I stared at Wreight. "Surely that includes this as the knife the witness *saw* . . . ."

"Absolutely not," Fred snapped.

"Proceed, Mr. Campbell," Klezky growled.

"Ms. Biagi, is this the knife you saw?" I placed our exhibit on the wooden ledge between the witness chair and me. Motionless, she stared at it as if the knife might slither off the ledge.

"Can you answer, Ms. Biagi—is this the knife you saw?"

"Well, it looks *like* the one that Mr. Burnell held."

Turning from the backhand slap I felt across my cheek, I saw the ghost of doubt start whispering into Klezky's ear.

As I feared, on cross-exam Wreight opened with a salvo emphasizing how our switchblade "only looks *like*" what she'd seen.

Then he exposed the other soft spots in our case: how crowded was the bar, how many people sat or stood between Biagi and Burnell, how dim the lighting was.

The waitress came across as honest, trying to be accurate, revealing no bias or hostility. As his finalé, the attorney asked her once again if she could swear Exhibit A was the same knife she saw.

Innocent as custard pudding, Biagi turned to face the judge: "Well, it *sure looks like it.*"

Wreight had fallen in the classic self-created trap of asking one too many questions. "Nothing further from this witness," he sighed and settled in his chair.

"Prosecution rests," I snapped as if Biagi's last four words had stamped out any doubt about our case.

Responding to his lawyer's nod, defendant shuffled to the witness chair. Twenty-three years old and six-feet-two, Burnell would box as a heavyweight.

He took the oath and ardently denied he had a knife that night. What he'd turned back to get when he was told to leave was a bottle he'd brought with him to the bar.

Wreight looked at me: "Your witness, Mr. Campbell."

That's it? That's your defense? You'll fight hell to make that fly; in fact your client is about to meet a lawyer straight from hell.

Warrior, feeling confident, urged me to do more than poke holes in defendant's claim; instead go for Burnell's throat. But this reminded me of how a prior would-be mortal blow backfired when I'd tried it in a jury trial.

Fighter pushed away this thought: *Today there's only kick-ass Klezky to convince, not jurors who might swoon with sympathy when you play too rough with an accused.*

I felt sure Burnell was lying. But I didn't have a previous conviction to impeach his credibility or an absolute I.D. to wind into a knock-out punch.

So I opened with a question aimed at casting doubt that a saloon would let its patron bring a bottle in and leave it on the bar.

"I don't know why—they just let me," he replied.

Growing bolder, fighter risked a "why" question—one whose truthful answer I could never prove. It would give Pinocchio a chance to grow his nose. But first I opened up the knife and placed it gingerly upon the edge of Klezky's bench as if it were a ticking bomb.

Q. Mr. Burnell, why didn't you just leave the bottle in your car?

A. Uh . . . I thought they might not have my brand.

Oh man, you're airy as a bag of butterflies!

Q. So, you claim you only held a bottle, not a knife that night?

A. That's right.

Q. Then what happened to your bottle when the waitress yelled, "He's got it again!"?

A rope of silence snaked around defendant's neck.

A. Well, er . . . I must have handed it to *friends*. I guess, *they* must have taken it.

"No further questions for defendant," I announced.

In summation for the judge I emphasized the lack of prosecution bias in our witnesses, how the officer at first even agreed to let defendant leave.

I pointed out that Kienan only busted the defendant when he heard Biagi shout, "Look out, he's got it again!" and saw him make a backhand gesture towards the ground. A switchblade was the only item on the floor, lying right at Burnell's feet.

I added that, unlike most excited eye-witnesses to crime, Ms. Biagi didn't swear Exhibit A was *exactly* the same knife. Yet she was confident the switchblade gleaming on the judge's bench "*sure looks like it.*"

Wreight's summation underscored each doubt arising from a case where no one unequivocally observed his client with Exhibit A. "Your honor, think how many other patrons could have dropped that knife inside a dimly lit and crowded bar."

As I rose to make rebuttal argument, I felt the need to bolster prosecution's case, secure its tapestry inside a stronger frame. I tried a thought-experiment I wouldn't dare with jurors. I suggested Klezky weave together the most likely threads of Burnell's and our versions of this incident.

"Your honor, if you do, you'll see defendant carrying his knife, not a bottle, to the bar on 13th Street. You'll see him stashing it, perhaps beneath a napkin, maybe in the gutter of the bar, when the officer arrived. That's what he turned back to get when he was told to leave."

I sat down trying to look confident and hide my apprehension that the ghost of doubt had made a nest inside the judge's head. Klezky cleared his throat and voiced my greatest fear: "I've got a nagging doubt," he said, "concerning the possession of Exhibit A. . ."

He reached for the switchblade on his bench where I had stationed it. He grasped it, turned it over in his palm, and stared at the defendant. ". . . but in all fairness I conclude my doubt is just not reasonable. . ."

Mergot and I faced each other, trying to suppress our grins. Warrior gave out with a soundless whoop.

24

"...Therefore I find defendant Darnan Burnell guilty.
Sentencing to take place one month from today."

* * * * *

Personal reflections I wrote after every trial pointed to this
case's ironies: In court Burnell stretched his credibility
beyond the breaking point with his brought-in bottle claim.
In the same way he had stretched his luck by turning back
to get his switchblade from the bar.

If he'd decided not to take the stand, my case would have
reeked with doubt. But his implausible defense became the
choke point of this trial; it throttled Klezky's qualms about
his innocence. This time the ghost of doubt that haunted my
last trials did not get the final hoot.

That night Dru and I dined out on halibut and joy. I'd won
my premier courtroom victory for the government.

But just before dessert Drusilla bounced her brows at me:
"Art, did you get your rush today from seeing justice done or
from feeling you had won?" She knew how single-minded
her ex-pugilist could get inside a ring.

"Both," I said and held her gaze to show I'd answered
honestly.

But she'd raised a point that needed further scrutiny. I
would only face it squarely near the end of my career as
counsel for the government, the day my fighter would
convict a man who actually was innocent.

TRIAL BY SURPRISE

Most of life's significant events take us by surprise.
—Source unknown

After winning yesterday, I roared the rattletrap Camaro
through blazing autumn leaves and into work. I was keen to
plunge into another trial. Instead our democratic roster
detoured me to "calendaring court."

* * * * *

Calendaring Court: Its purpose was to gather all the
misdemeanors set for trial that day, determine which were
ready, and assign them to a judge. Depending on the
number of arrests one month before, between thirty and fifty
trials were calendared each day, to be dispersed among two
dozen courts.

It was a challenge to corral so many counsel, cops, and
witnesses inside one room. Dealings there resembled cattle
calls for casting C-grade films.

My job as prosecutor was to synchronize our office files with
those of the court and make sure our witnesses had shown.
Standing at the front of the largest courtroom in the
courthouse, I manned a podium inside the "bar" that
separates the public from their law.

Listening for the clerk's announcement— "U.S. versus
Hurley Slickensides" —I would finger through my cardboard
box of upright files and pull the one that matched
defendant's name. I'd peer at entries on the outside of our
file to see which witnesses were cops, which ones civilians.
Then I'd turn around and scan the courtroom, looking for
some gesture from these folks.

If I caught a nod, hand wave, or rising torso, I'd make eye
contact, lift my chin and brows to signal, *Are you ready?* If
their non-verbal cue was yes, I'd turn back to the judge and
sing out, "Ready for the government."

Warrior basked in puff-points from this public show of
power, but the administrative exercise did nothing to

enhance my trial skills or give me opportunities to practice freedom law.

When defense was also ready, the presiding judge would nod to his clerk, who'd dispatch the case for trial with a randomly selected judge.

I would hand our file to the arresting officer, who took it to the trial court and gave it to a prosecutor waiting there. That courtroom's judge either tried the case or—more likely—entered judgment in accordance with a bargained plea.

A deal might have previously been struck between our office and defense, or get quickly parlayed moments before trial. Sometimes the tipping point to plea wasn't reached until that morning when defendants saw our witnesses had actually appeared.

* * * * *

My first day in calendaring saw two-hundred people packed like Pringles in the courtroom's gallery. Judge Harvey Stormhold kept the chaos to a jostling, softly mumbling mass.

I had argued many motions before Stormhold when I worked for the defense. He was a dynamic and no-nonsense sovereign of whatever court he ruled.

I also pegged him as a "freedom judge." That meant he rigorously enforced the Bill of Rights and tailored sentences to rehabilitate, not turn offenders into warehoused savages intent on vengeance when released.

This made him a rarity inside the District of Columbia, where black robes showed more wear from leaning toward the prosecution's side.

Today the clerk himself sent all ready cases to a courtroom to be tried. Judge Stormhold only weighed in when he saw that one side or the other was unprepared for trial.

Then he berated lawyers, witnesses, and cops—whomever was to blame—and only granted a continuance when some essential soul had been detained inside a jail, hospital, or morgue.

If the government could not produce its witness or a good excuse, Stormhold showed his fealty to freedom law; he dismissed our case. If defense was to blame, he reset the trial date and banged out warrants to arrest the witness, the accused, or the attorney who had failed to appear.

By noon today Stormhold had assigned nearly all our forty-seven cases. As I shifted weight from one collapsing arch to the other, it felt good to know my work was almost done. Stormhold recessed court for lunch til one p.m.

Bird songs laced my amble to an outdoor restaurant four blocks from the court; a tired toy balloon tiptoed in the gutter by my feet. Along with tasty food I hoped this place would serve fresh scenes devoid of nervous litigants and lawyer folk.

I finally had the chance to munch a lunch without recalling morning testimony or strategizing for the afternoon. Until today trial-prepping seemed to beateth me beside the stillest waters.

Sitting there, I watched a guy attack his steak big as a catcher's mitt while his girlfriend rescued carrots from a bowl of gumbo. Both snatched glances of themselves in the reflective restaurant window. Inside, a one-eyed television peered down at a dozen tables of cud-chewing prey.

I sat back in my chair, relishing a hot-pastrami sandwich and slow sips of Guinness beer. *Ah, remember how it was to lead a normal life?*

But I lingered there too long and had to lope back to the courthouse in my grey-tweed suit. I leapt inside the elevator's closing jaws but felt them stutter to a stop one floor short of calendaring court.

Judge Stormhold—six-feet tall, two-hundred pounds inside the billows of his robe—marched in. "Enjoy your nooner, counselor?" he grinned as I dragged a handkerchief across my sweat-streaked brow.

Before I could respond, he said, "We're close to done with calendaring. What say you to a little bench trial we can finish by this afternoon?"

"That's great by me!" I said, my R.P.M.s still bouncing in the red.

The government had charged George T. Braeker with two counts of D.D.A. (Dangerous Drug Act) for both possessing and distributing desoxyn, an amphetamine known on the street as "bam." Judge Stormhold soon dispatched all other cases to be tried except this one.

The jurist looked down from his bench. "Mr. Braeker, will you confer with able counsel and see if you would like to waive a jury and try your case before me at this time?" Although Stormhold smiled broadly, the defendant's neck sank into his shoulders like a rabbit trying to look small.

Sitting next to him was counsel Sarah Cottlinger, early thirties, long brown hair. A faint ring at the bottom of her skirt showed she'd dropped its hem from days of shorter styles.

Cottlinger was struggling to maintain a landlord-tenant practice, now and then augmenting it with criminal defense, two distinctly different specialties.

I reached for our office file while she grabbed Braeker's arm. I heard them murmur furtively like two guests at a funeral. "You should seize the chance to try your case before a good judge for defendants."

"Okay, if you say so," Braeker said.

Stormhold turned to me. "Mr. Campbell, it looks like your witnesses are here. I'll give you five minutes to decide which one to call first."

My hot flash of nerves was quickly seered by warrior's adrenalin. *Just my luck—another damned possession case! At least today my witnesses are cops or chemists. Let's see if I can steer this case into another win.*

Stormhold riffled papers while I stepped behind the rail to confer with two narcotics cops. The third witness was our chemist; he dropped me a nod and moved with his metallic briefcase to the gallery's front row.

Overflowing in the morning, the courtroom now was occupied by less than twenty spectators. "Routine bust," the first narc whispered, briefly filling in the whens and wheres. His partner added, "Yup, that's right. Saw it all as backup."

"Ready for the government," I said. "Ready for defense," responded Cottlinger.

Officer Duncan Haggis took the stand and, after stating name, job, and experience, began his narrative. Four weeks ago he and his undercover partner eased through a pool hall in a "high narcotics area."

I visualized the smoky rundown place where last year as defense attorney I had served subpoenas, glad to be accompanioned by my buff investigator.

Haggis was the kind of cop who by-passed the vernacular to boost his credibility. He didn't say he "saw George Braeker dealing drugs." Instead he "observed defendant" with "three other individuals" on the "premises" where "said subjects" were "exchanging money for some merchandise."

When both plain-clothed narcs approached, the group dispersed and Haggis saw their suspect shove his hand inside the left-front pocket of his slacks.

Haggis and his partner seized defendant ("placed him into custody"), cuffed ("restrained") his hands behind his back, and reached into his pockets ("conducted inventory of his personal effects"). Haggis grabbed ("retrieved") a palm-sized plastic envelope, housing 17 orange tablets of suspected bam.

30

All possession facts established for the court, I took my seat. Cottlinger arose for cross-exam.

From our office file I knew she had confronted Haggis at a prior hearing in this case. Seeking to exclude the tabs as fruits of an illegal search, she'd lost that motion. I figured she had tried but failed to kick a dent in Haggis's testimony.

Today she launched an energetic sally into details of the bust, seeking to ensnare the narc inside some hoped-for contradiction of his prior words—to prove that either this time or before the man was "testilying."

Frustrated by his self-assured responses to eight rapid-fire questions, she shook her head and took her seat. Her client frowned and stared two lasers at the narc as he stepped from the witness chair.

I called the second officer and he confirmed what Haggis said. On cross-exam Cottlinger again fell short of prying up some warped or splintered testimony.

During my direct of both narcotics officers, I'd asked if they had seen defendant giving or receiving any plastic bags or tablets in the hall. "No," they'd candidly replied.

I wondered why our office even papered "distribution" in this case. Some recent law-school graduate—no doubt thinking of his class on circumstantial evidence—must have figured 17 desoxyn tabs were more than one guy needed for a day and papered Braeker with intent to deal.

That raised another irony: Braeker might have pled to mere possession—saved taxpayers both a hearing and a trial—if someone in my office had volunteered to vacate the distribution charge. I would have proposed this deal if I'd been given time to probe more deeply in this case with the two narcs.

Before Judge Stormhold could dismiss the distribution charge for lack of evidence, I said, "For the sake of justice the government now moves to drop the dealing count."

"Granted," ordered Stormhold, "just in the nick of time." He banged his hammer, flashing me a toothy grin.

I recalled the rush my freedom lawyer felt on day one as a prosecutor when I no-papered a detective's charge. Today was another first, exercising freedom law in court.

My last witness was the chemist who had tested samples of the tablets seized from Braeker. I went through the standard litany of questions on his education, expertise, and analysis of drugs, now marked as government's Exhibit A. Then I pounded in my final nail. "What did your tests conclude about the nature of those tablets in Exhibit A?"

"They clearly were desoxyn—an amphetamine."

"No questions for this witness," Cottlinger announced and made a backhand wave.

My case in chief was done. What could this defendant do to wriggle off the hook?

George Braeker strolled to the witness chair, raised his hand, and took the oath. All he had to offer—but he did with bold defiance—was to swear his bams were legal, that they'd been prescribed.

Cottlinger sat down. "Your witness, counselor," said Judge Stormhold, looking solemnly at me.

My fighter rubbed his palms together, eager to attack. I first exposed defendant's inability to give the full name of his doctor or the whereabouts of the physician's clinic, office, hospital, or home.

Next I asked if he would show the court a copy of his doctor's scrip. He shrugged and said he'd "lost the paper somewhere in Virginia during my arrest down there for something else."

During each admission Braeker's cocksure attitude dropped a cog. Soon his chin sagged like a child after waves had washed away his castle in the sand.

Before I finished cross, I asked Judge Stormhold for two minutes to confer with the narcotics officers. Mindful of my first two trials—where I'd failed to stamp out smoldering doubt—I asked my seasoned "team" what they could add before I laid our trial's outcome on the platter of a pro-defendant judge.

I was happily surprised when Haggis told me Braeker testified before that he had found his bag of bams just lying in the street!

Indeed, stapled in my file was a transcript of defendant's prior testimony. *All right! I'll blast him with this contradiction. If need be, I can follow up with both detectives' testimony that they'd seen no prescription when they'd searched defendant's clothes.*

But I faced a legal pitfall. I could not use defendant's words against him when they'd been spoken in a hearing to suppress. It would be unconstitutional to force a man to choose between his Fourth Amendment right to testify pre-trial about a cop's allegedly unlawful search and his Fifth Amendment right not to be incriminated when those words were flung at him in trial.

If Stormhold saw me flout this basic principle, I knew he'd lose his temper, call a mistrial, and set Braeker free. He might even hold me in contempt, as he'd done before to lawyers for the government.

I addressed the judge, acknowledging I knew the protocol. "Nonetheless," I said, "the Supreme Court has recently permitted an exception to this rule—to show defendant lied."

"Mr. Campbell," Stormhold warned, "you may proceed, but cautiously."

"Mr. Braeker, did you testify at a suppression hearing in your case two weeks ago?"

"I strenuously object!" cried Cottlinger, apparently not knowing of the recent case.

"Forget it, both of you," Judge Stormhold said. "Under New York versus Harris, Mr. Campbell only has to introduce the transcript."

So I did. Stormhold scanned its pages, stopping at a place that made him purse his lips. "Ms. Cottlinger, since you were there, I presume you know exactly what your client said. Mr. Braeker, do you care to tell me why you told a different story then—or do you wish to exercise your Fifth Amendment right to silence now?"

"Your honor …!" Cottlinger exclaimed, apprehension blistering her face. But as she stammered to collect her thoughts, her client waved her off.

"Your honor, I lied back then to save my brother. It was his prescription for the bams. I got them off of him."

"No good, Mr. Braeker!" boomed the judge. "I believe you're lying now. Unless there's further defense evidence or argument, I find defendant guilty of possessing an illegal drug with no prescription in his name."

Cottlinger sat back and shook her head, her expression like a half-dropped pie. Braeker shrugged his shoulders, turned, and watched a maple tapping leafless twigs against the courtroom's window pane.

Warrior clenched a victory fist beneath my desk as two marshals handcuffed Braeker and escorted him from court. *You've notched another prosecution win, and from a 'defendant's judge'!*

On my prosecutor's list of virgin victories, this was my debut trial for drugs, first time I'd dropped a charge mid-trial, first in which I'd "qualified" a chemist as an expert witness, and the first time a defendant copped to lying under oath.

As I walked to my office, I pondered charging Braeker with two counts of perjury—only one of his three stories could possibly be true. Then I heard the echo of my wife Drusilla's voice: *Hey, you're really thinking like a prosecutor! But does your warrior's rush from winning now outshout your call to freedom law?*

Denials tumbled from my mind: *Hadn't I dismissed one unsupported charge and carefully avoided trampling Braeker's constitutional rights?*

But freedom lawyer closed the argument: *Hey, baseball man, you got your hit; you needn't try for extra bases. Let the poor guy take his lumps for D.D.A.*

So that day warrior won the argument in court but not along the hall. And all I thought I'd fight were fallen arches in a court of calendars!

LOOKOUT SPROUTING DOUBTS

Behind every great man is a criminal.
—Dostoyevsky

One autumn afternoon Darnell Curtz and Eddie Banner walked into a Dart Drug store. The first man lugged a sturdy plastic box of magazines still smelling of their printer's ink.

Curtz was eighteen, slim, and six-feet-one. At twenty-three, Banner stood a pudgy five-foot-nine. They worked for a distributor of periodicals, replacing all outdated magazines with current ones.

For three years Carlotta Dobbs had stalked Dart's aisles as an S.P.O. (Special Police Officer, i.e., private guard.) She'd watched Banner restock magazines a score of times before.

But she'd never seen him bring a partner, let alone a handsome hunk like Darnell Curtz. Casually she glided down the shampoo aisle, keeping both men in her sights.

Curtz paused beside the rack of magazines, set down his bright red box, turned to an adjacent shelf, and reached for Brut cologne. He unscrewed the cap, smelled the fragrance, sealed the bottle, and gave it to his partner. Banner dropped it casually into their box.

Dobbs edged closer for an unobstructed view. What she saw next triggered her adrenalin. Curtz looked from side to side as Banner stepped up to a rack of tape cassettes, grabbed a dozen, shoved them deep inside their plastic box.

The men exchanged expired magazines for new ones, piling last week's LIFEs and TIMEs atop the Brut and tapes. Curtz picked up the box and both men sauntered from the store.

Dobbs signaled a cashier to phone D.C. police as she trailed her suspects to their car. When Curtz heaved the box inside the trunk, Dobbs reached in her jacket and withdrew a snub-nosed thirty-eight.

36

Uniformed police arrived and carted off both men. Because the value of the goods was relatively low, they were booked for petty theft.

Our office could have upped it to conspiracy. But we reserved this felony for intrigues larger than a bottle of cologne and tape cassettes. We charged each with misdemeanor larceny, which also let them ask for separate trials. They did.

One month after their arrest, I was assigned to try all misdemeanors sent to Judge Rao Goodyear's court. Detective Dobbs walked through the doorway at 9:40 in the morning, introduced herself, and handed me our office file: "U.S. versus Darnell Curtz."

As I absorbed the file's contents, my confidence began a heebie-jeebies dance. A minefield of distractions lurked beneath the surface of this case.

For me distractions were facts not strictly relevant to guilt but packed with power to seduce a juror's mind. They were invitations to ignore the law and follow fitful sympathies.

It had been defendant's first day on the job; he'd never met his partner til the day of their arrest. After checking out the incident, their boss had fired Banner yet mysteriously retained the new guy, Curtz.

What magic cloak protected Darnell Curtz? What or who convinced the company to let him keep his job? The answers could blow up my case. How could I prevent them from exploding in the jury box?

The courtroom clerk informed me Curtz's lawyer was before another judge where he would need another quarter hour. I walked downstairs to our office, found a more experienced colleague, spread my file and misgivings on his desk.

"It's tough, Art, but go ahead and give it your best shot. Emphasize how Curtz was lookout for his partner in their larceny. That makes him flat-out an abettor. Make sure jurors get instructed on that point."

Reaching in my briefcase, I snagged my standard jury instructions clutched inside red–binder claws. I dog-eared the page on aiders and abettors.

As I marched back to court, warrior pumped me up: *What a challenge this case is! Think how good you'll feel if you win.* Freedom lawyer also tossed me reassurance: *At least you've not been sent to prosecute a guy who's innocent.*

When I'd switched to prosecution from defense, I'd settled on a strategy if I were pressured to convict someone I thought not guilty. I'd take the file to my boss and argue we should drop the charge. If he disagreed, I'd smile and say, "Then please pick someone else to try the case. If I can't prosecute with *personal* conviction, I won't try the case at all."

But Curtz's case was not like that. I had no doubt about his guilt—just qualms that I could sell my picture to a jury of his peers.

My doubts doubled when Curtz's counsel strode into the court. At thirty-eight, neatly tucked inside a tailored suit and gleaming shoes, Charlie Fiece had earned a place among D.C.'s top trial lawyers. *Curtz's family must have paid a bundle for your services!*

Fiece approached me, smiling like a candidate for office. I shook hands, equaling his power-squeeze, and wondered, *Was it your juice that got Banner fired while saving Curtz's job?*

Judge Goodyear entered through a door behind the bench. Handsome, forty, wearing wire-rimmed glasses, his constant smile signaled he enjoyed his job. He was a homerun searching for a small ballpark.

I gave my jury opening without using notes. I pitched a preview of my case, starting every wind-up with "The evidence will show ..." I laid out all the segments of the S.P.O.'s surveillance up to Curtz's bust outside the store.

Fiece rose after me: "The evidence will *also* show . . . ," he said, and lit fuses of distraction all around my infield.

He said his client was a poor boy of the projects, scraping first-year fees for college from a part-time job. In the drugstore on his first work day, he didn't know his trainer meant to *steal* anything until they reached the parking lot. By then it was too late; the S.P.O. had drawn her gun.

Freedom lawyer slapped his hand on fighter's arm before he leapt up to object on grounds these facts were irrelevant. Fiece could counter-argue they related to his client's state of mind—that Curtz was too naïve to harbor criminal intent. Fiece was sharp enough to think of that response.

Besides, my protest might make jurors think I'd try to keep them in the dark about the nature of a man the government accused of crime. So I stayed rooted to my chair; this was not a hill I chose to die upon.

My only witness was Detective Dobbs. I called her, asked her to identify herself, and tell the jury what she'd seen the morning of the incident.

"Objection!" shouted Charlie Fiece, quick as a slap. "Improper direct examination."

"Sustained," ruled Judge Goodyear. "Mr. Campbell, you mustn't let a witness ramble with a narrative. You must ask her questions point by point."

"Ms. Dobbs," I asked, "When did you first observe defendant, Mr. Curtz?"

"Objection, leading question! Plus, there's no foundation that she'd *ever* seen my client, Mr. Curtz."

"Sustained," said the judge.

Now fighter seethed: *So, my learned friend, this is how you play the game. Despite my merely setting up the scene,*

*you'll throw dust each time you get a chance. Even D.C.'s best
will stoop to sandbox lawyering if he thinks it helps his side.*

"Your honor, will you insist defendant's counsel be
consistent? First he wants me to focus witness testimony.
Then he complains when I comply."

"Quit bickering, Mr. Campbell, and get on with your case,"
responded Goodyear, no longer smiling.

*Okay, fighter thought. That showed the jury someone in this
courtroom isn't awed by Charlie Fiece. Now it's your turn,
judge, to show you've got a backbone underneath your
robes. Let Fiece know his stature as a legal lion won't make
you blink each time he kicks a little sand.*

For the rest of my direct of Dobbs, I used the tiny trowel of
courtroom protocol to scoop a narrow path between
unguided narratives and leading questions: "Then what
happened?" "And did there come a time when . . .?" "What, if
anything, did you see next?"

Fiece crouched on the front edge of his chair—his jaw
clenched like a trigger finger.

Eventually I reached the place where I would ask the clerk
to mark a lock-sealed envelope for evidence as government's
Exhibit A.

Lock-sealed envelopes had strips of paper glued across their
paper lips, initialed by the latest sealing officer. They could
not be opened without severing the strip, an act saved for a
mini-drama moment inside court.

After showing Fiece the sealed envelope, I placed it on the
ledge in front of Dobbs. She identified the packet as the one
in which she'd placed the stolen goods from Banner's trunk.
I asked, "Since then, has the seal been broken?"

"Objection!" yelled attorney Fiece, lunging from his chair as if
to save the world from imminent collapse. "There's no way
she can tell if that seal has been broken and resealed."

40

"Rephrase, Mr. Campbell," ruled the judge.

I felt round-housed by an iron boxing glove—I'd heard my routine question asked a score of times in court and never draw objection.

Judge Goodyear's will of tissue had been swept away by Fiece's babble brook. Now the jury might suspect we'd tampered with the trial's crucial evidence!

"Mr. Campbell, please proceed," intoned the judge sardonically.

Were qualifying questions for an S.P.O.'s lock-sealed envelope different than the ones for normal D.C. cops? Whirling through a roulette wheel of other ways to ask this question, I chose red-number-four: "Ms. Dobbs, does the package *appear* to be unbroken?"

No objection from defense. I'd found the Northwest Passage for our envelope.

I labored through a dozen more procedural objections as I forged a chain of custody for the purloined tape cassettes and Brut, backtracking and rephrasing questions with painstaking specificity.

Goodyear finally let my witness break the seal on her envelope before the jury's straining eyes. As Dobbs peered inside she gasped, "It's gone! The *cologne's* gone!"

I approached the witness, trying to disguise the uppercut slammed in my gut. Doubts were sprouting from this trial like mumps on a toad; now they could taint the S.P.O.'s entire testimony.

Trying to look confident, I plunged my hand inside the envelope. Fishing through the plastic boxes of cassettes, I felt my fingers close around the Brut; I pulled the bottle out.

"Ahh, there it is!" Dobbs said; then she released a loud sigh of relief. Jurors smiled and sat back in their creaking chairs.

Leapin' lizards—this kind of courtroom drama I can do without!

Directing Dobbs through her next phase of testimony, I stubbed my toe against another point I'd never seen arise in court. My goal was to establish as an element of larceny that the Brut and tapes were taken from the store without permission of Dart Drugs.

"Officer Dobbs," I asked, "do you know if anyone at Dart that day said it was okay for Darnell Curtz and Eddie Banner to cart away those goods?"

"Objection, calls for hearsay!" clamored Fiece, vaulting from his gulch of gab.

"Sustained," said Goodyear. "Rephrase, Mr. Campbell."

"Ms. Dobbs," I asked again, "As an *agent* of Dart Drugs, do you know if defendant had permission to remove the goods in question?"

No objection from defense. *Banged away that curveball, Fiece!* Then a squadron of misgivings jetted through my mind.

I wondered whether Fiece was turning off the jury with his pettifogging interruptions of my case. Or did jurors relish watching his exhibit of a "vigorous defense?"

Is warrior's lust for victory blinding me to what is really going on inside our jurors' minds? It takes only one distraction to taint their brains with doubt—and distractions have been blowing through this case like billows of unholy smoke.

I scrolled through a mental checklist to make sure I'd brought to light all elements of larceny. Had I proved Curtz "took possession and carried away personal property of another without consent and with intent to steal?"

Yes, I muttered to myself, fired a look of calm assurance at the jury, and announced, "The prosecution rests."

Instantly Fiece moved for acquittal based on lack of evidence. I felt a frisson of relief when Goodyear ruled there was enough to let our jury do its job. It was now defense's turn to build a case.

When I sat down I knew, except for cross-exam and summing up, the fight was almost done. *Not won, just nearly done*, my warrior's voice reminded me.

Fiece called his client to the stand and kept his promise to supply the jury with "the facts they'd need to reach a proper verdict in this case."

Using words from Curtz's mouth, Fiece slammed Eddie Banner as the only guilty man, the person who got fired, the "job-boss" his client was compelled to follow to the parking lot.

It grew clear the only way I'd win this case would be to prove that Curtz had been a volunteer conniver and was now a cunning liar. I had to make his naïve-victim image melt like cake left in the rain.

But in addition to outstanding preparation for his client's direct testimony, Fiece had home-schooled Curtz on how to handle cross-exam.

I hammered at the man for thirty minutes but couldn't crack his image of a struggling, would-be college student on day one of work. He still came across as a youngster who'd been duped to help his boss swipe cheap items from a giant drug-store chain.

I only struck two dents in his veneer of innocence. I had him first assure the jury that he'd told them "absolutely everything you did inside the store." Then I got him to concede there were two items he'd "forgotten to include."

He admitted he had watched his cohort hide the Brut inside the plastic box. And, yes, he'd looked from side to side as Banner likewise grabbed and stashed away the twelve cassettes.

Would those aiding-and-abetting acts turn our distracted jury to the view I held?

In summation, Fiece's and my own portrayal of events were so unlike that jurors must have thought we'd watched two different videos.

Mine focused on the theme that Curtz knew from the start what Banner planned to do and freely served as his shoplifting lookout.

Fiece portrayed his client as a trusting, callow youth, forced to walk beside "the only culprit in this case." Banner was the man who "really stole the goods and was fired just as he deserved."

I admired my opponent's casual finesse: *This man could sell burnt matches to a firebug.*

Jurors caucused for two hours and chose defendant's video. I shook Charlie Fiece's hand. "Nice job," he said, magnanimous in victory.

It's a rum day when you lose, warrior mumbled angrily. But having faced all those distractions, I knew his pride would manage to survive.

Driving home that evening through a rumbly thunder storm, I sifted out some lessons from the day. Overall my win-loss tally grew one worse and yet my courtroom skills had grown considerably.

With only twenty minutes prep I'd tried a jury case, conducted opening, summations, direct and cross-exam—all without support of notes. Plus I'd gone toe-to-toe with a premier trial lawyer in D.C.

Forty minutes later I pulled in the driveway of our cottage in Virginia's countryside. I wished Curtz luck in college; today he got the freedom he would need. But it was I who got a post-grad education course.

JUST KNOCK IT OFF

Once you're a trial lawyer you're addicted. It's like smoking,
or any other habit-forming act. You get hooked on
cross-examination like you get a taste for great gulps of fresh air.
                                                    —John Mortimer

Today I was again dispatched to try all misdemeanors in
Judge Goodyear's court. He remained in chambers while I
waited in his courtroom for a case to come our way.

I debated Forty-Niners' football with the bailiff, and our
forecasts for a sky whose bloated clouds refused to rain.
Then I huddled with a set of earphones at the prosecutor's
desk and listened to taped lectures about California law. I
was cramming for the Golden State's intimidating bar exam
a few weeks down the road.

I snapped in and out of daydreams where I practiced in a
San Francisco office lined with walnut bookshelves, leather
chairs, and Berber rugs.

Behind me the door banged open. Twisting in my seat, I saw
a D.C. cop stride through. He smiled while approaching,
shook my hand, and smacked a file folder on my desk.

"Name's Jorge Lattimire, the arresting officer. We've got a
double drug-bust here." It was the first I'd heard of Ulna Reed.

* * * * *

Reed had been halted in a supermarket when her tendered
check matched one on a list of *DON'T ACCEPT*. The
cashier thumbed a button underneath her counter,
summoning the manager. He invited Reed into his office
near the produce section of the store.

Police were also called. Her arrest would send a warning to
the neighborhood of what happens to repeated paper
hangers in his store.

When officers arrived they placed the contents of Reed's
shopping bag along the manager's desk. At the bottom were

three one-inch tinfoil wraps of heroin. So they dumped her handbag. Out rattled five loose "bams"—amphetamines, unlawful to possess unless prescribed.

Since Reed, aged thirty-three, had no record of arrests, we declined to yoke her with two counts of dealing drugs, sentences for which could age her twenty grey-bar years.

Instead, the chief papering assistant decided we should charge her with two misdemeanors, one for possessing each illegal type of drug.

Holding heroin was filed under U.N.A. (Uniform Narcotics Act); the amphetamines fell under D.D.A. (Dangerous Drug Act). Both carried a potential year in stir. The chief concluded these were tough enough to overlook her crimes of bad-check and attempted larceny.

He was doing more than sprinkling mercy on defendant's shopping bags. The twin charge was also crafted to induce her guilty plea: "We'll drop one count if you'll plead guilty to the other."

But this incentive failed. Reed trumpeted her right to freedom law: She pled not guilty, got a court-appointed lawyer, and demanded that we prove she knowingly possessed illegal drugs.

Since she'd lost a prior motion to exclude them as unconstitutionally seized, how could she block the fact her shopping bags contained both drugs? Warrior buckled on his sword and said, *Looks like an easy win.*

* * * * *

Again the courtroom door swung wide: entered Larry Witcar. A fortyish Fifth Streeter with a dark blue blazer punctuated by a red bow tie, Witcar wrung his livelihood from court-appointed indigents.

The lady in his wake was clad in stylish sable slacks and cerise nylon blouse. She shot a glare at me that could nail horseshoes to a tree. The woman must be Ulna Reed.

"Ready for trial,"Witcar warbled in a casual tone. "Mrs. Reed prefers to save the court some time and waive her right to have a jury hear this case."

"Thank you, Mr. Witcar," said the clerk. "Will you have your client autograph this waiver form? Mr. Campbell, how long before I call the judge?"

"Just long enough for me to use your phone and call our chemist from his lab. How's that?"

"Fine," the clerk replied. Like most sergeants who know they really run the army, she was conscious of her power. "Your chemists sometimes take a while to get to court. So you'll call the officer as your first witness?"

"That's my plan."

Five minutes later Judge Goodyear entered from a door behind the bench. His thick neck hinted at a stocky body under his cascading robe.

I drew the judge a verbal sketch of what our evidence would show and motioned Lattimire into the witness chair. He described where, when, and how he'd found the heroin and bams.

The officer related how he'd placed each drug inside a separate lock-sealed envelope, both of which he'd brought to court. I introduced them into evidence as government's Exhibits A & B.

Our chemist eased through the courtroom door just as Witcar rose to cross-examine Lattimire. I flashed the man a thumb-and-finger "O," relieved that he'd arrived in time.

Witcar's questions bunched around a single point: his client had cooperated during every stage of her arrest.

Our chemist took the witness chair and swore the drugs he'd tested were those now nesting in the envelopes I handed him. Exhibit A contained the heroin; B held the amphetamines.

"No questions for this witness," Witcar chirped without glancing from his notes.

What's going on? Where's his defense? Has Witcar stashed a witness in the hall? Or did he catch a client who distrusted him, wouldn't let him cut a deal? That would clear up why he seemed afraid to say hello or even look at me when he walked into court.

Warrior shoved aside this speculation: *Just bring it on. I can't wait—whatever that phrase means—to bag an easy win.*

But freedom lawyer felt a tickle-cough beneath his fighter's confidence: *Art, have you forgotten that there ARE no easy wins in misdemeanor trials?*

I skimmed a mental list of elements I had to prove: *Yes, I've hit each one.* I looked at Goodyear and announced, "The prosecution rests."

Witcar clambered to his feet as if he couldn't wait to take command. But he didn't make the customary motion for a judgment of acquittal based on insufficient evidence. Instead he said, "Your honor, the defense calls the defendant, Mrs. Ulna Reed."

Imperiously she strode across the hardwood floor; her chin was raised as if she feared her eyeballs otherwise might tumble from her skull.

With slow enunciation, Reed related her address and gave her occupation as a "part-time stylist of hair." She declared she and her husband were hard pressed to "raise our sixteen-year-old son inside the projects, judge. We're trying to keep him out of trouble through uneasy times."

Okay, ma'am, power to your parenting, but what the hell is your defense?

Reed cleared her throat: "Judge, I know how those tinfoil packets *must* have gotten in my shopping bag. Just before I went to the cashier, a man from the projects walked up and said he'd help me with my groceries. At first I thought, 'He's acting mighty strange, especially for a guy who deals heroin'."

Reed shifted in her chair: "But then my bag *was* heavy and I didn't want to make him mad. So I said, 'Sure' and handed it to him. He must have dropped those packets on my groceries—maybe 'cause he feared that he'd get caught."

Aha, another version of I-didn't-know-the-thing-was-loaded! But you can't make that glider fly. Lattimire already testified the heroin was found *beneath* your groceries, not where it would have been if dropped on top or even thrust along one side.

A week before this trial, I'd finished Wellman's classic, THE ART OF CROSS-EXAMINATION. It suggested lawyers should *not always* bring out damning points on cross, but save them for another part of trial.

Should I question Reed about the placement of that buried contraband? No, I'll follow Wellman: use it later in summation when she can't dodge this contradiction to her tale.

Reed continued: "Now about those pills inside my purse. My husband is a big-rig driver. He's on the road a lot. He gets drowsy but he's got to keep on driving to his stop. I'd gotten a prescription filled to help him stay awake. So all those pills were legal, judge. Here's their container with the doctor's scrip."

Reed unzipped her purse, fished inside, and came up with an empty plastic vial. A prescription was clear-taped to its sides. She thrust it towards the judge.

Goodyear raised both palms to the defendant. Turning to attorney Witcar, he asked, "Counselor, have you looked at this?"

"Yes, your honor."

Goodyear turned to me, "Have you seen it, Mr. Campbell?"

"No, your honor. May I?" The jurist nodded for his bailiff to convey the vial to my desk. I looked it over. Fighter muttered, *Reed, your story's tangled as a trunk of wire coathangers.*

I plopped the container back into the bailiff's calloused hand. He conveyed it to the judge.

Goodyear took the vial, read the label, and placed it on his bench. "You may proceed, Mr. Witcar."

The lawyer asked, "At this time, Mrs. Reed, is there something else you'd like to tell the court?"

She crossed her arms atop an ample bosom and responded, "No, that's all."

"Cross-examine, Mr. Campbell?" asked the judge.

I rose and aimed my chisel at the weakest link in her defense. "Mrs. Reed, are you aware the label for your husband's medicine is dated three weeks *after* your arrest for this offense?"

A. "Well, I . . . What? . . . How can that be?"

Judge Goodyear looked again at the container. He slid his chair on its five tiny wheels toward the witness chair and handed Reed the bottle. Her brows furrowed as she squinted at its side.

Q. "And did you know the medicine on that prescription is for a *different* kind of drug than the amphetamines found in your purse?"

Her haughtiness imploded like a jack-o-lantern two weeks after Halloween. "Oh my, I must have mixed up the containers. I *had* a vial just like this, your honor. I brought the wrong one in today. The pills they found inside my purse must have slipped from the container with the right prescription on its side."

Warrior clenched his fist: *Mrs. Reed, you're all cowboy hat— no cattle—and you're branding non-existent steers.*

I could easily recall my officer to prove there'd been no vial or physician's scrip inside her purse. He could add she didn't volunteer this explanation at the scene or station house. Since both demolition tools were handy if I needed them, I decided I would risk a courtroom demonstration.

Q. "Mrs. Reed, can you show Judge Goodyear how the lid of a child-proof container can accidentally come off? Will you take your vial and knock the top off with your hand?"

Firmly grasping the container in one hand, the defendant used the other like a hatchet, striking upwards at the lid. It didn't budge.

She bit her lip, changed her grip, and struck another blow. The third time she turned the vial bottom up and whacked her fingers down its side. The lid remained in place. She stared at it despondently.

"No further questions for Ms. Reed, your honor." She stepped down from the witness chair, this time firing me a look that could have lasered steel.

Part one of my summation felt like an anti-climax. I merely pointed out the obvious: Uncontroverted presence of illegal drugs in Reed's possession; the tiny likelihood that foils of heroin could find their way *beneath* her groceries; the container she produced was not for bams and was dated post-arrest.

Witcar stood behind his desk and argued abstract principles of doubt—not once referring to his client's testimony. Suddenly the shape of his defense snapped into place.

Attorneys may not foster perjury but defendants have the right to testify. There's a classic resolution to this head-on clash of lawyer ethics and the Constitution: Lying clients are allowed to take the witness chair but their attorneys can't direct them through a narrative or later base an argument upon suspected perjury.

Clearly Witcar had decided he must walk the tightrope stretched between these poles. Even with no credible defense, he had to honor the defendant's right to have a trial, take the oath, and try to sell her bogus tale.

In rebuttal I reminded Goodyear that our testifying officer had said nothing of discovering a container or prescription in defendant's purse. Even had a vial been there, Ms. Reeds' claims about its spilling were disproved by all her efforts in the witness chair. My focus on her story's contradictions let me duck directly calling Reed a perjurer.

I sat down and, along with others in the courtroom, stared at the judge for his decision in the case. He stalled, rearranging papers on his bench.

Her guilt is clear as sunshine! warrior urged. Freedom lawyer also felt a prosecution verdict would see justice done.

I wondered at the impact of attorney Witcar's ethical gavotte before the bench: *How can Goodyear reach a realistic verdict in this case and not be conscious of the lawyer's silent signal that his client lied?*

Judge Goodyear never aired how he arrived at his result. Declaring Reed was guilty on both counts, the jurist simply said that he believed the testimony of our cop and chemist, finding the defendant's explanation was "inherently incredible."

Instantly my fighter felt a rush from his favorite home-grown drug: the adrenalin of triumph. As I repacked my briefcase, I reflected on the day.

I hadn't overcome a feisty foe or pasted hasty patches on a leaky prosecution boat. Indeed, it was defendant's skiff that had dissolved into a sieve. But I'd put Wellman in effect and dared to make a courtroom demonstration demolish the defendant's claim.

As I marched to our suite of offices, my tachometer still cha-cha'd in the red. Warrior prodded me: *Why don't you stick a note inside the file? Shouldn't you alert whomever gets this case for sentencing that Reed may try to float her cock-and-bull accounts again before another judge?*

Since you asked, responded freedom lawyer, *why not let her try to sidestep Stony Lonesome, snag the usual sentence of probation for a first-time misdemeanant in a case without a victim? You've won your guilty verdict—why kick her when she's down?*

In duels between my warrior and my freedom lawyer, fighter often won. Not this time. I placed Reed's file on the table of our office manager.

"Guilty on both counts," I said and walked away.

A JURY OF ONE'S PEERS

There are two theories about how to argue
with a judge. Neither works.
—AWC

My most challenging experience as a prosecutor wasn't
packaged as a trial. It was a hearing that consumed six days
in court while spanning seventeen across a calendar.

* * * * *

Weeks before, another prosecutor was assigned what seemed
a simple drug-possession case. The judge was Horace L.
Bachover, one of only three black-robers in Superior Court
known as a "defendant's judge."

This tag meant he took an active role protecting people's
rights; he practiced a judicial form of freedom law. Not that
every other judge espoused the prosecution's side.
Although many did, most merely took a neutral stance,
leaving constitutional and other rights in the hands of
counsel for defense.

Before my colleague's trial actually began, Bachover
vanquished every would-be juror over forty years of age. He
declared too many senior citizens paddled in the jurors' pool,
depriving young defendants of a jury of their peers.

By coincidence Bachover's act had been inspired by a
complex motion filed months before in federal court by
attorney Lois Goodman. At that time I'd been her co-counsel
for defense.

The U.S. Attorney was appealing Bachover's dismissal of
older jurors, arguing essentially his absence of supporting
facts. The judge had scrapped time-honored protocol
without a penny-weight of evidence.

As this appeal was pending, Bachover was assigned another
young-defendant case, the one that would eventually be mine:
U.S. versus Wolcott Carver.

Carver was accused of stashing heroin inside the zippered lining of his leather belt. On the jury-composition issue, the only crucial fact was how long Carver had been breathing on this earth; his age was twenty-two.

Once again the judge proclaimed his aim to edit elders from the panel til the jury box was filled with only Carver's "peers." But this time the jurist vowed he'd craft a factual record to support his goal.

Our office first assigned Glen Flinder to this case. In the middle of Glen's voir dire of potential jurors, Bachover said he'd take "judicial notice" that the average D.C. juror's age fell somewhere between forty-five and fifty years. (Later evidence would boost that age to fifty-one.)

Thereupon the judge gave counsel for defense and prosecution one week to brief all points of fact and law to ascertain what is a jury of one's peers. But three days into this continuance, Glen was transferred out of Washington, D.C.

Word spread around our office that I must know a lot about this subject because of my defensive days with Lois Goodman. Summoning "poetic justice," colleagues joked that I should be the one to throw a prosecution lasso over all the issues Lois prodded into life.

The day before Thanksgiving my boss called for me. Clovis Bankwood placed the Carver file in my hand: "Not only should you be familiar with defendant's point of view, but Bachover might even like you since you used to help him get so many guilty people off our hook."

I didn't tell him it was Lois who'd unearthed the law and facts, wrote the motion, and presented witnesses to back it up. I also doubted that my former role would quell Bachover's fire-breathing tirades against prosecutors.

But I was proud that Bankwood trusted me to build a solid record for the government's appeal. We both knew I'd lose the hearing in Judge Bachover's court.

So, while friends and jurors of all ages crunched through another holocaust for turkeys, I fought the blues and blahs behind a thankless desk at home. Bachover had ordered legal memoranda to be filed the day after Thanksgiving.

Using Lois's photocopied motion as a guide, I tried to block or tackle every issue for the team of Uncle Sam. After I wiped gravy off a bunch of drafts, my memorandum stretched to fourteen printed pages.

I filed the memo Friday but knew it wouldn't mesh with every fact in Carver's case. Since I'd not been in court to hear what had been said, I had to cast my arguments in abstract form. It felt like breathing life into a mannequin, then stepping back to fence with him.

Three days later I obtained a transcript of all previous proceedings in U.S. versus Wolcott Carver. I stuffed it in my briefcase and hiked four blocks from our offices to Georgetown Law School's library. Pulling my first load of books from musty shelves, I stacked them on the table like a just-sliced loaf of bread.

I spent six hours searching law, mainlining coffee, scanning slowly blurring print. My mood trudged along a cobbled lane of boredom, doubt, discovery, and silent cheers.

Filling reams of pages from two yellow pads, I worked a beaver's day, consuming woodlands slice by slice. I emerged with thirty more sub-issues, factual and legal, that a court must master on this multi-level mountain of constitutional law.

More importantly I climbed to an overview. All issues fell in line behind a basic three: How *did* the District of Columbia choose its pool of jurors? What *was* the age that satisfied the law for peers? Do trial judges have discretion to *create* that kind of jury?

I also glimpsed a fundamental difference between Bachover's aim and the one that Lois Goodman framed. Goodman sought a negative solution: Invalidate the system citywide until it got repaired. Bachover's goal was positive: Mold a proper jury for each accused inside his court.

Freedom lawyer now grew keen to litigate these novel points. He trusted that the trial court would gather all the facts and legal principles at stake. The final rule of law could then be laid down by *appellate* courts.

Fighter was excited to cross swords with counsel for defense and an active trial judge. He knew Bachover wouldn't buy his basic argument that jurists shouldn't tailor juries to the age of a defendant. So warrior also was content for vindication on appeal.

My strategy in Bachover's domain was simple and low-key: Support the government's position with solid evidence and not waive a legal issue by not raising it.

* * * * *

Tuesday after Turkey Day I made my first appearance in the courtroom on this case. A jam-packed briefcase brushed against my thigh as I climbed the marbled stairs to court. Its signal to my left hand—*All prepared*—always gave my fighter confidence.

Before the judge arrived I introduced myself to counsel for defense. Roshman Saunders was a man in his mid-thirties, average height, and black receding hair. Three months earlier he'd moved to D.C. from a New York civil law career.

He confessed to scant experience in court, plus barely making it financially. He'd joined the ranks of Fifth Street lawyers, those who lived on court-appointed cases, shilling guilty pleas instead of vigorously protecting clients' rights.

Despite my view that Fifth Street lawyers slithered lower than shoelaces on a snake, Roshman and I remained congenial throughout this case. Sometimes we stood as cohorts when Bachover's temper rained judicial cloudbursts over both of us.

When the hearing started, neither Saunders nor I had an inkling that its hours would continue to expand like stretching segments on a cartoon caterpillar.

At nine a.m. Bachover made his entrance into court. Handsome, tall, grey temples gracing middle-age, his flamboyance and defense of people's rights made him a champion of the D.C. populace.

But he was also volatile and quick to take resistance from attorneys as a personal attack. Assignment to his court was seen by colleagues in my office as a call to fence with Satan on whatever ledge the jurist chose to make a stand.

Citizens in court were all upstanding as Bachover's clerk intoned, "U.S. versus Wolcott Carver." Abruptly Saunders seized the podium and blurted out, "I apologize, your honor, but I only got a copy of the prosecution's fourteen-page memo last Friday, and haven't yet been able to research or file a response."

Bachover's eyebrows dropped like awnings right before a storm. His voice was preternaturally calm. "But today is Tuesday, Mr. Saunders. So, your client's interests and this court are not worth your effort?"

"I don't mean that at all, your honor," Saunders minced. "It's only that I've got so many cases before so many other judges that . . ."

Bachover roared, "Counselor, please inform this court which case or judge is more important than your duties here!"

"Oh, absolutely none, your honor." Saunders tucked his chin and shifted weight from one foot to the other.

"Then you'd better get to work and take these jury issues seriously. This court has raised them for your client and you act like you don't care!"

"I *do* care, your honor. I just need more time."

"Mr. Campbell," the judge turned predatory eyes on me. "Are you prepared to offer evidence supporting all the points raised in your memorandum?"

"I'm prepared to argue points of law, your honor. But it's the government's position that defendant has the burden to place facts before this court that prove the current system's flawed."

"*I* raised the issue, Mr. Campbell!" bellowed Bachover. "It's the *court's* proposal to correct a problem it regards as totally unconstitutional, one striking at the heart of trial by jury in our nation's capital."

The jurist paused, searching for more words. I braced for the attack. "Mr. Campbell, you're an officer of the court, and I instruct you *now,* to bring in any evidence you think can reinforce the government's position that the D.C. system rests on solid ground."

Suddenly Bachover clutched his chin. He grimaced, "Counselors, you're both in luck today. The court has a toothache that needs immediate attention. We stand adjourned until two days from now."

* * * * *

At the appointed time I waited at my desk in court. Three prosecution witnesses perched behind me in the gallery. I'd located and persuaded them to come without a hint of my subpoena power.

That contrasted with defense attorney days and what it often took to get witnesses to court: a subpoena in their hand and a ride in my investigator's car. Now I only had to lift a phone and mouth the magic mantra, "Hi, I'm an Assistant U.S. Attorney for the District of Columbia."

At 10:15 Bachover entered with a flourish of his robes and dropped into a judge's swivel chair. He trained his brown-eyed tractor beams at Saunders: "Is counsel for defendant ready to proceed?"

"Yes, your honor," Saunders said, then glanced apologetically at me. "Uh... defense calls Mr. Greystone, a jury commissioner for the District of Columbia."

Although taken by surprise, I didn't mind that Saunders called "my" witness. Both sides needed to create an accurate account of how jury candidates were rounded up from all the precincts in D.C.

But I feared Saunders might mess up this job since he hadn't prepped the witnesses—as I had—nor was he a seasoned courtroom questioner.

I didn't worry long. Each time Saunders' queries missed their mark, the judge—eager to create a pedestal of data for his later jury sculpting—leapt in to solidify his base.

On cross-exam my chisel merely cleared out curly chips, making sure each image of our transcript's verbal picture had clear edges for appeal.

But just creating a foundation out of facts—a task I thought would take four hours—consumed five courtroom days. Our reporter began stacking transcripts into multi-volumed books.

On day one I volunteered to schematize what I saw would soon be overlapping testimony on the way the city gathered juror candidates. I brought in a large, blank, cardboard poster, drew a flowchart in black ink, and invited witnesses to place different colored numbers on it corresponding to their testimony.

On the second day, fighter prodded me to make a slip in strategy. Remember thirty new sub-issues found from further research? Freedom lawyer should have filed a supplemental memo, disclosing them and how they neatly stacked beneath a fundamental three.

Instead warrior wielded them like playing cards, clasping each behind his adversarial shield, only flashing one when it

could capture useful evidence. He scoffed at greater candor:
Turning cards face-up is for dummies playing bridge.

This strategy kept attorney Saunders constantly "defensive."
But it also kept Bachover in the dark. "Well, Mr. Campbell,
why didn't you inform the court about *this* issue," he would
chide each time I asked a witness questions to support some
unrevealed legal point.

On day three of the hearing Bachover turned to the
defendant. "Mr. Carver, you're looking bored and I don't
blame you. I'll grant you bail on personal recognizance
although your counsel hasn't asked for it. And I'll excuse
you from appearing til this motion is wrapped up. But
keep in contact with your lawyer, so you'll know the date
your heroin-possession trial will commence."

Good move, freedom lawyer said. *All this legalese must
interest him like fruit salad does a tiger.* It was the last time I
saw Wolcott Carver.

Earlier, Bachover had ordered one of "my" witnesses, a
computer-analyst, to run a program that would find the
median age of D.C. residents. Today the number-cruncher
would undergo cross-examination on his quest.

As both counsel and his honor fired questions at the man, we
discovered that his figures didn't rest upon a proper
population base.

This set off Bachover's anger, which he flung with equal
fervor at Saunders and yours truly. Somehow we had "kept
this witness from producing crucial information for the
court!"

I choked fighter's urge to point out it was he who yesterday
had framed the expert's faulty program. ("Sir, will you write
down this formula for your computer run?")

The witness rubbed a thumb along his pen as if it were a
genie's lamp. He must have felt yanked head-first through a

privet hedge. *I'll bet he's mulling that programmer's axiom: "Garbage in means garbage out."*

After a free-wheeling colloquy among the judge, Saunders, and me, Bachover ordered the beleaguered man to return next day with data from another program we three non-computer specialists devised.

Day four came and, after spreading new statistics on the record to our satisfaction, we let the number jockey retreat to non-litigious life. He audibly exhaled as he dismounted from the witness chair.

By that time Saunders and I had jointly interviewed staff members of the Jury Commission. Bachover accepted into evidence our stipulation of procedures by which jury pools were siphoned out of population reservoirs.

Then the judge surprised me. He gestured to a well-dressed, middle-aged female in the audience. Inviting her to take the witness chair, he introduced her as "an expert for the court."

A clinical psychologist with prominent credentials, she cited lengthy studies to support her ultimate conclusion: "People over forty have a hard time grasping what life means to people around twenty years of age."

So, what else is new? fighter thought, remembering his parents from the Pleistocene. Then I realized Bachover wanted evidence that older jurors would be *prejudiced* against the twenty-two-year-old defendant in this case. However, it felt unfair the judge had failed to warn me that this witness would appear.

On day five another fin cut through the surface of courtroom collegiality. This time without notice Saunders brought an expert in.

The witness was an eminent psychiatrist, although his pin-striped suit had fit him better twenty pounds ago. His testimony struck the bull's-eye of Bachover's target: Older folks, he swore, were "simply biased against youth."

Holy Hannah! warrior thought. *Here endeth all our prior good will and collaboration. This must be payback for my fighter's hiding those sub-issues earlier. Had Bachover or Saunders warned me of these witnesses, I could have questioned them strategically.*

Effective cross-exam of experts requires knowing everything they've published, said in public, or in court. It also needs researching other sources who might modify or undercut their views.

To counter experts who knew truckloads more about their fields, at least warrior had to cloak his questions' aims. But my attempts to do this often coiled questions into such complexity both witnesses claimed they couldn't understand what I had asked.

Twice I turned and confidently asked the court reporter to read back my question. Hearing my own words, I realized they'd zig-zagged down a cake-walk of tautology. But when I rephrased, my goals became so obvious the witnesses made sure I never made it near the touchdown zone.

After vainly struggling with each expert, I resumed my seat, trying to conceal my simmering frustration. I'd failed to expose one blemish in their logic or its base in solid research. Nor had I raised a single bias or self-contradicting stance.

Warrior jabbed me in the ribs: *Besides more time for specialized research, you need more practice on your feet, cross-examining experts.*

Day six in court saw Saunders and yours truly finally summarize our views. I argued thirty minutes, using notecards spread across my desk. My bottom line was that judicial tinkering with a jury's age would be unconstitutional.

With surprising ease I managed to extract supporting evidence and testimony from files in my litigator's ad hoc memory vault. Through it all Bachover sat upright, locking eyes with mine.

Saunders spoke for twenty minutes, glancing over pages of his legal pad. But each point he made drew nods of acquiescence from the judge. While agreeing with the facts I'd stated, Saunder's legal argument spun a big 180: It would be unconstitutional *not* to shape a jury of his client's peers.

Although I'd strained to mold persuasive arguments, backing each with facts and legal principles, I held no hope of courtroom victory. Bachover seemed determined to fulfill his role as savior of the D.C. jury-trial right. He merely needed factual support so he could stride across a choppy legal sea.

After luncheon recess—filled with mental replays and analogies I should have used—the time arrived for Bachover to make his ruling in this case. His first words astonished me.

"This court finds itself without authority to interfere with jury composition by striking members on the basis of their age."

Without a glance in my direction, he continued: "To do so would indulge in discrimination just as arbitrary and unconstitutional as basing strikes upon religion, race, or sex."

To my unbelieving ears he added, "Though I find the D.C. process of locating and selecting jurors unconstitutionally discriminates against our city's youth, this court will not apply the maxim 'two wrongs make a right'."

I sat immobilized, trying to maintain a poker face and snap a tether on my leaping warrior. *Bachover bought my arguments!*

It seemed the more miraculous because his ruling flew directly in the face of all his ballyhooed intentions that he'd mold a jury of defendants' peers, followed by his five-day round-up of supporting facts.

This bombastic egotist had weighed his personal ambitions against opposing legal principles and actually reversed his course! Seldom had I witnessed transformation like this in a public figure, especially one with such discretionary power.

But Bachover's work was not yet done. Now he had to wade back through our testimony and statistics and state for an appellate court which ones he found accurate. Stopping now and then to peer at notes he'd scribbled in his judge's book, he labored to complete our record with official facts.

As I listened to his findings, I wondered if there were other ways he could have reached his goal. He might have voided the entire jury-gathering process as unconstitutional until repaired; this was the solution Lois sought.

But that would generate two kinds of heat I doubted Bachover could tolerate. He'd likely be assigned no jury trials until the matter was resolved months later on appeal.

And he might ironically be headlined as *THE JUDGE WHO STRUCK DOWN JURY TRIALS IN THE DISTRICT OF COLUMBIA*.

Just then I heard Bachover inadvertently transpose two crucial numbers from our computer expert's testimony. I rose to my feet.

"Mr. Campbell," the judge growled, grumpy as a snake-bit bear, "after you've prevailed on this motion, do you have the gall to interrupt the court?"

"I don't mean to interrupt the court, but just point out that . . ."

"So you *do* have something you think more important than the findings of this court?"

"Of course not, your honor. I only wish to help the court to . . ."

"So you believe this court needs help from counsel for the government?"

"Absolutely not, your honor."

"Then sit down, Mr. Campbell."

I sat but kept on talking in a placatory tone: "I only want to make sure your record is protected from a switch of two important numbers which I'm sure your honor didn't mean to make."

Bachover roared, "Stand up, sir, when you address the bench! *That's* what you had to say? *That* was more important than the findings of this court?"

I rose again: "Not at all, your honor."

"Sit down, sir!" Bachover ran a finger down one page of his judge's book. I sensed the rocket of his temper start to level off. With less vigor he complained, "Sir, you've totally derailed the court's train of thought."

Not really. He picked up his narrative precisely at the place where he'd left off, then carefully back-tracked to change the numbers he'd transposed.

My six-day joust with Bachover was done.

* * * * *

Office colleagues yelled, "You're kidding!" when I told them I had won. But Bachover's clerk phoned confirmation to my boss; Clovis Bankwood called me in.

"Congratulations, Art—you just accomplished the impossible!" Both fighter and my freedom lawyer beamed. At last I felt accepted as a member of the team, a *real* prosecutor.

Then he asked, "How'd you like to be assigned the next two weeks to Bachover for trials? You seem to thrive inside the devil's lair."

I paused.

Bachover was a blustery curmudgeon but he was a "freedom jurist" too. Plus his high-bar standards for the prosecution made his courtroom an ideal training ground for me.

However, I had sweated through my meager courtroom wardrobe: one blazer and two suits. I needed time to shake off sixteen days of stress and let my outfits travel to and from the cleaners.

"Boss, give me a week to try some misdemeanors with another judge. Then I'll take Bachover on again."

That night, driving home along the pike, I sped by new construction sites; they grew like giant weeds on what had once been rolling hills. I thought about the crop of new experiences springing up around my life.

As I maneuvered the Camaro through a stretch of thick Potomac fog, distant pictures wafted through my mind. I reflected on pre-litigation days: horse-back riding, camping, reading poetry, hanging-out with my bolero bride.

Since those days of fun and happenstance, I'd been the willing captive of research and writing, daily deadlines, trial preparation, and outcomes out of my complete control. I'd lived inside adrenalin arcades of court appearances, each closing with the kick of instant victory or defeat.

I heard a small voice whisper, *Is this the way you want to spend the balance of your life? Today you loved this litigation feast, but would a lifetime bring contentment to your soul?*

At that point in my career I answered, *Yes*—spurred by fighter's lust for battle and freedom lawyer's call to duty. It would take a few more years before my soul would finally shout, *Enough!*

* * * * *

Bachover's name still reigns atop my list of favorite jurists. How many judges will reverse their publicized designs because of logic or the law?

Another colleague from my office took over U.S. versus Wolcott Carver. Strange, I never asked how it came out. Odds were the defendant pleaded guilty—which, of course, would moot appeal of the jury-system issues we had aired so thoroughly.

Nor, as weeks went by, did I hear any other court—local or federal—declare that D.C.'s jury-composition was unconstitutional.

But months after Lois Goodman's prolonged hearing for defense and mine for the government, a news item caught my eye. The D.C. jury commissioner had called a conference for the press.

He'd decided to reform a juror-finding protocol that now seemed out of date. Henceforth, juries in the District of Columbia would contain a larger number of the city's youth.

TOSSED-HEROIN DEFENSE

Communication is basically verbal
but comprehension is essentially visual.
—Steven Lubet

Next week, a time of sodden autumn leaves, my boss
assigned me to the court of Ulster Caravelle. I'd try all
misdemeanors dispatched to the smallest courtroom in D.C.
Measuring 40 feet by 60 feet, wall-to-wall green carpet
undergirded a new jury box and judge's bench, both of
polished oak.

Like a mini-movie-theater, it elevated intimacy above
intimidation. Even tables for opposing counsel were
obliquely angled so, like friends, they nearly faced each other.

I liked the relaxed atmosphere but wondered if its coziness
would dim a jury's deference to law. A surprising answer
came at trial's end.

Of two counsel tables in a courtroom, prosecutors always
seized one closer to the jury. Today as I walked in, I staked
this territory with my legal pad and briefcase. The jury box
gleamed a mere four feet behind my chair.

When jurors later took their seats, fighter hoped this
placement sparked subliminal images: I'd be the pilot of their
plane, coach of their athletic team, director of their choir.

Once warrior thought of scribbling large letters on my legal
pad: *HE'S GUILTY!* or *HE'S LYING!* At some strategic point
in trial I'd casually plop the tablet on my table in the jury's
view. Freedom lawyer put the kybosh on that fancied scam.

A uniformed policeman strode through the courtroom door.
Five-foot-eight with blonde Marine-cut hair, he vise-gripped
my hand and beamed a victor's smile.

"I'm Hans Stagwort, the arresting officer in a case of holding
heroin." Handing me our office file, he *soto voce'd* his
synopsis of the facts.

Looks like a lock, my fighter thought, *a winnable possession case!*

Again the courtroom door swung wide and Scot Brickyear strolled inside, clad in the light-brown suit he wore to court each day. He was a mudder of the Fifth-Street tribe, lawyers renting tiny offices beside the court; their specialty was talking clients into guilty pleas.

In his early sixties, Brickyear's skin would win trophies at a cactus fair. With a constant look of discontent, he pled ten defendants guilty for every one he took to trial. Today I watched his hapless client being sandwiched through the door by two grim U.S. marshals.

I leafed through the file Stagwort handed me. The defendant's name was Thatcher Davenport; Brickyear obviously had failed to bail him out of jail. It was typical neglect, the kind that kept Fifth Streeters barely dodging missiles of malpractice.

I squinted at the lawyer and his client as they whispered to each other, forearms leaning on their counsel table. *Brickyear, you old mossback, why did your hibernating morals choose to take this case to trial? You've either got some weird defense or your client choked on a plea-bargain you tried cramming down his throat.*

The lawyer seemed to read my mind. Turning toward me in his chair, he whined, "Sorry, Art, my guy won't plead. Won't even waive a jury for a trial by the court." He could have sounded more contrite but not without a new prescription from his cardiologist.

"No problem," I replied, disguising my disdain for lawyers who apologized for guarding a defendant's rights. He didn't want to tick me off for fear I'd harden the next bargain for his overloaded ferry full of court-appointed fares.

Warrior leapt on Brickyear's diffidence. Smiling like a happy cobra, I asked if he'd stipulate the case involved heroin of a "usable amount." This fact is usually uncontested; we could save the time of all concerned.

But I blundered making my request in earshot of his client, instead of drawing Brickyear to one side. "Hell no!" hollered Davenport. "I'm stipulating *nothing* in this case." His stare telegraphed if I dropped dead he'd dance with joy.

Turning from his client's view, the old sheep raised his brows to me, signaling his helplessness. He epitomized a Fifth Street lawyer's oxymoron: The job would be much easier without a human client.

Judge Caravelle walked slowly into court. He was a slim man in his fifties with a regal bearing crowned by salt-and-pepper hair. Twenty-five non-adversarial minutes was all it took to pick twelve jurors and two alternates.

Brickyear waived his opening and I called Stagwort to the witness chair. He introduced himself and described his duties as a plain-clothes officer. Explaining how he'd spotted Davenport on Eighteenth Street, he portrayed the crucial scene.

"From ten feet away I observed two tinfoil packets in defendant's hand. When he saw me look at him, he took off in the opposite direction, ran five steps, and slammed into the side of a parked car. As he fell he tossed the packets on the street. I picked them up four feet from where he lay."

Stagwort opened a lock-sealed envelope and displayed two shiny packets in a plastic bag. I had the bag identified as government's Exhibit A.

For cross-examination Brickyear raised his butt an inch above his chair and asked a single question: "Officer, when you first saw my client you didn't know for sure if he had heroin in his hands, isn't that the truth?"

The seasoned cop replied, "Each packet was the normal street-size used for heroin but, no, I wasn't positive until I had them tested in our lab."

All right, Stagwort, smack him and our jury with a little extra evidence!

As Brickyear settled at his desk, I called our laboratory chemist to the stand.

* * * * *

I need to sketch a little background here.

Before technicians give results of tests, the trial judge must certify them as forensic experts. Since each case has different jurors, witnesses must be recertified for every trial.

Our office kept a list of expert-qualifying questions up to date, so we'd track ever-changing standards from appellate courts. For reasons lost in time, we called our question list a "gouge sheet."

These stapled pages guided prosecutors to elicit the technician's education, training, and experience. They prompted us to mention every link along a chain of custody that towed Exhibit A from the arrest scene to the lab, to storage rooms for evidence, and now to court.

Finally the gouge sheet guaranteed we'd bring out laboratory tests that leapt through current scientific hoops. Only then could we request the expert to divulge what kind of drug the tests revealed.

* * * * *

As our chemist took the oath, I flipped through our file to retrieve the latest gouge sheet. Silently I cursed whomever papered charges in this case. The klutz had stuffed two scripts inside—without marking which was obsolete!

In order not to skip some crucial qualifying point and risk reversal on appeal, I held a script in either hand, asking every question from one sheet that wasn't on the other. *Better err on too much information, than leave out something critical.*

My Q-and-A was so *pro forma*, neither Brickyear nor the judge objected to the lengthy dialogue. Some jurors' eyes began to glaze.

At last I reached my goal. "Does Exhibit A contain the drugs that tested positive for heroin?"

"Yes sir," the man replied. Without rising from his chair, Brickyear cavalierly said, "No cross," as if the chemist were irrelevant.

My third witness was a narcotics cop. With a shorter gouge sheet I qualified him as an expert on the street use of illegal drugs. He summarized his formal training and two years working in the D.C. addict scene. He verified defendant's heroin was a "usable amount."

Again Brickyear punted cross-exam.

I asked Judge Caravelle to admit as evidence the tinfoil packets in Exhibit A. No objection from defense.

"Your honor, the government rests," I said. Warrior wondered if this phrase arose from days of sweaty knights on horseback, needing breathers after their initial charge.

Attorney Brickyear rose, turned to the jury, and dramatically announced, "Defense calls its single witness, the defendant, to the stand."

My fighter sneered, *Stands disappeared a hundred years ago, Brickyear. How many pages of your mind are stuck together? At least you manage to avoid a senile drool.*

I dug into another section of my file, one with the defendant's history in our system. Instantly I saw why Davenport had not made bail: Ten days ago he'd been convicted of armed robbery!

Nervous as a deer on ice, Davenport crossed the courtroom and eased into the witness chair. He wore a polo shirt, black chinos, and new sneakers—not a jumpsuit of electric orange, that year's sartorial standard in the D.C. Jail.

At least someone gave you good advice: don decent street togs for the jury, so you don't look like a rock-pile candidate.

73

Davenport's defense, rambling and disjointed, congealed into two essential chunks. First, "some guy shoved those packets in my hand just before the officer arrived." Second, "I didn't know what was inside but was scared it might be bad. So when I saw an undercover officer, I ran. When I hit a car and fell, I threw the stuff away."

Warrior scoffed, *that cheese won't travel far. Surely street-wise jurors won't buy your "some guy" story. Even if they do, it's no defense. Au contraire, you just admitted to possessing heroin!*

On cross-exam I started, "Sir, are you the Thatcher Davenport who was convicted ten days ago in D.C. Superior Court of armed robbery?"

He shot me a locked-down look. Trial lawyers welcome anger in an adverse witness; it can twist their logic, shatter shields hiding truth. "No, I'm not that man," he scoffed.

All right! fighter crowed, *now you've stepped in your own mess.*

My file held a certified copy of his conviction. With it I could double-slash his credibility: once for a crime of "moral turpitude," another for denial of that guilt.

But as I dove for the certificate, I heard freedom lawyer warn: *Don't let fighter goad you into overkill as he did that day when your impeachment triggered jury sympathy!*

So I didn't ask the killer-question, "Isn't it a *fact* you were convicted of armed robbery ten days before today?" Nor did I introduce my document to prove he was a liar.

Instead I asked Judge Caravelle for permission to approach the witness chair. I placed his record of conviction in defendant's hand. "Does this *refresh your recollection*, Mr. Davenport?"

"Well . . . yes . . . I *was* convicted of armed robbery. But it wasn't just ten days ago!"

Maybe he was thinking of the time he *did* the crime, not the day he pled. Regardless, I decided not to spar with him on this unimportant detail. I simply sat and let his quibble bounce around the down-sized courtroom's walls.

When it was time for final argument I made sure my fighter's feelings rested firmly in a saddle of restraint. I held back from boasting of my airtight case or shoveling sarcasm on a ludicrous defense.

I trained a spotlight on this trial's two key facts: (1) Defendant was arrested "silver handed" with two packs of heroin; (2) he testified that he'd possessed the drugs. "What more do we need to know?" I asked rhetorically.

Brickyear's arguments were merely variations of "Are you really sure you should convict this man?"

What's he mean by that? What else is there to this simple case? With no contradiction from defense, how can that pesky ghost of doubt find a roost inside the jury box? But fighter grew a little nervous fencing with a foe whose face remained concealed.

I pried apart the claws of my red binder, lifting out approved instructions to the jury about drug-possession law. Without objection from defense, Judge Caravelle charged the jury from my sheets.

At 4 p.m., twelve upstanding citizens single-filed out the door, leaderless until they picked a fore, and straggled down the hall to their deliberation room.

Davenport retired to the courthouse lockup, escorted by another brace of marshals. Brickyear sidled over to my desk, eager to agree our jury would be back inside an hour, so obvious was his client's guilt. Instead of going to our offices, we waited in the courtroom.

At 5 p.m. we were surprised to learn our jury hadn't reached a verdict. Caravelle told his bailiff to discharge them with an order to return at nine tomorrow and resume deliberations.

What kept them so long inside the jury room? Warrior
tried to dance a jig of confidence but felt like he was
stuck in vichyssoise.

Next morning at 11, my office telephone called me to return
to Caravelle's courtroom. Twelve jurors trooped back to
their box and asked the judge if he'd repeat his earlier
instruction on "possession."

*So that's what got them arguing! It's clear as a shout: they
want the legal meaning of the word so they can silence
someone's cockamamie notion from the street.*

Caravelle said they needed to determine if defendant had the
power and intent to control a useable amount of heroin.
When three jurors nodded knowingly, my fighter, like a
football fullback, waited for his hand-off five yards from the
end zone, feeling paydirt almost underneath his feet.

At noon I was sorting through some office paperwork when
my phone yahooed me back to court: our jury finally
reached a verdict.

All parties reassembled, Davenport beside his counsel, waiting
for one word to add another year to his armed-robbery time.
Warrior stood behind the prosecutor's desk, ready to be
gracious for his fish-in-barrell victory.

"Not guilty!" boomed the forewoman. The faces of two
lawyers, one defendant, and a judge froze into flabbergast.
The Blindfolded Lady winced.

I approached the bench. "Your honor, would you ask *how*
these jurors found defendant did not hold illegal drugs? It
would help us all to understand this case."

Judge Caravelle, veteran of litigation wars, said, "I think I
know what went on inside the jury room. Let's see if I'm
correct." He thanked the jurors for their service, then asked if
they'd participate in an experiment "just for fun."

The forewoman scanned her colleagues' faces and responded, "Sure, your honor."

Caravelle tore a sheet of paper from his legal pad, scrunched it to a crinkly ball, and threw it on the floor four feet from his bench. "Am I guilty of possessing that paper wad?" he asked the forewoman.

"No," she confidently replied, "because you threw the thing away!" Eleven other jurors nodded their assent.

"Your honor," she continued, "in this case there wasn't any proof the stuff was heroin when the officer first saw him with it. Then, when the defendant threw those packets on the ground, he didn't have possession since, as you instructed us, he didn't have an intent to control. So at neither time did he possess what later tested out as heroin."

Judge Caravelle smiled patiently and dismissed the jurors. Brickyear slapped his beaming client on the back. Fighter gripped the backrest of my chair and ground his teeth, feeling powerless and angry as a drop-kicked armadillo.

Caravelle had clearly tracked the jurors' logic; so apparently had Brickyear. Once again warrior's lidless appetite had overlooked a jury's tendency to view the law through lenses of the street. He simply saddled up his steed and charged, blinkered by his blind belief that we would joust by *courtroom* rules.

Did a Fifth Street lawyer in an old brown suit steer his charger deftly down the *real* D.C. jousting scene? Did he later send a street-law ghost to carry doubt into the jury room? Is that why he never mouthed the word "possession"—out of fear I'd see that ghost and vanquish it in final argument?

Bowing to the hard rain of defeat, I grimly checked off "Yes" to all of the above. *What a lousy lawsy day—oh lawdy, am I lawded out!*

* * * * *

The consolation prize for placing second in a two-man race is the chance to learn some things. The lessons of today were not to underestimate a Fifth-Street lawyer and the way a jury can distort the letter of the law.

In my mind I heard the bass voice of my wisest client from defense attorney days. "Mr. Campbell, you need to learn to see the world through other people's eyes, including those of Fifth Street lawyers and the common folk of Washington, D.C."

Thanks, Cut, I responded. *But how could I miss their view about possession, one that seems so obvious now?* Cut said, "Remember when your wife and I once kidded you about idealistic arrogance and how it sometimes makes you miss what other people see?"

Oh my God, was that what...? "Yup," was Cut's reply.

The courtroom emptied, leaving only me—a sobered, lesson-learning lawyer—staring at the wall.

Fighter snapped me from my reverie. He vowed to my briefcase as I stuffed papers in its mouth: *This positively was the last time you will see me lose a damned possession case!*

But, before I zipped my briefcase shut, I heard a challenge from its closing row of teeth: *Hey, Art, want to bet on that?*

HEADS UP, OFFICER

The clearer a thing is, the more difficult it is to find any
express authority or any dictum exactly to the point.
—L.J. James

"Art, you've had your respite from Bachover. He's been
ripping our attorneys ever since you got the best of him," my
boss Clovis Bankwood said. "See what you can do to soothe
the savage beast."

At ten a.m. I stood again inside the court of Judge Horace L.
Bachover, watchdog of the people's rights, self-appointed
savior of D.C. from what he called "an over-bearing
government."

He had been assigned to try a non-jury misdemeanor:
soliciting for prostitution purposes—not a headline grabber
for the evening news, but my virgin sol-pros trial.

Defense counsel introduced himself: Nathan Cardot, student
in his final year at Georgetown Law. He was in a program
representing indigents accused of low-grade crimes. A thick-
necked blonde, Cardot looked like he once wrestled in the
ranks of college cruiser-weights.

Nipsy Murray, the defendant, glided into court as if she had a
jaguar on a leash. Lithe and twenty-five, she was sheathed
inside a leather mini skirt and creamy blouse with flouncey
sleeves. Without a word she took her seat at the defendant's
table, crossed her legs, and stared demurely, waiting for
proceedings to commence.

Blinds you with her science, I mused to my legal pad.

I knew Murray's chief defender would not be Cardot. Nor
would the real trial be the U.S. versus Nipsy Murray, but
Prosecution Lawyer versus Horace L. Bachover.

My challenge was to see if I could somehow wrest a guilty
verdict from his honor's likely pique with me and well-
known penchant to blast holes in prosecution proof.

From his churning entrance into court, "Let's get started, people," I saw Bachover's mood was teetering between feisty and perturbed.

"Mr. Campbell, I won't need an opening statement. Just call your vice-squad witness."

I summoned the arresting officer, Welter Clapp. Wearing blue slacks and a grey sports coat, he super-flyed across the floor and dropped his lanky body in the witness chair.

Clapp related his experience as a law-enforcement officer in Washington, D.C.: two years as a plain-clothes cop, the last nine months assigned to vice. Yes, he recognized Ms. Murray in the courtroom sitting next to her attorney.

I asked him to disclose the date, time, and place of his encounter with defendant.

"It was on November 10th this year at 4 p.m. on 7th Street, Southeast."

Q. Would you describe the circumstances?

A. As I drove my Monte Carlo slowly down the street, I made eye-contact with Ms. Murray. She was standing on the curb and gestured with her chin for me to pull aside. When I did, she leaned in the open window of the passenger door.

Q. And what, if anything, did she do next?

A. She exposed a generous amount of cleavage, smiled broadly, and asked, "Hey, sport, you up for a head job?"

Q. Based on your experience in vice, what did "head job" mean?

"Objection sustained!" roared Bachover before Cardot could jerk his head up from his notes. "Mr. Campbell, the court will recess for one hour. That will give you time to find authority for your last question."

Feeling walloped by a busted bag of bees, I dropped my hands and stared up at the judge.

"You heard me, Mr. Campbell," said the black-robed Doberman, quick to yank a meaning from the context of *my* stance. "Unless you find me some authority, I'll dismiss this case for failure to prove Ms. Murray's solicitation was for *sexual* purposes."

* * * * *

An hour later I returned with three ways I could squeeze "head job" into a sexual frame. Warrior smiled inwardly: *Let's see his honor play these tunes upon his anti-prosecution piccolo.*

"First, the government requests this court to take judicial notice of the term. It's not found in *LEGAL WORDS AND PHRASES*, but 'head job' is used so widely in our culture that the law permits your honor to accept the common meaning of this term."

Although my gambit was half tongue-in-cheek, I risked Bachover's wrath implying he should be familiar with the phrase. I was relieved to see a sparkle in his eyes when he asked with mock ferocity, "Do you mean I should possess *personal* knowledge of that term?"

"Of course not, your honor" neither as participant nor witness." I paused to gauge his next reaction. When he grinned, I added, "The government is merely drawing on your role as leading citizen in the community, one attentive to the meaning of the words he hears."

"So, Mr. Campbell, that's your authority, me? Is not this court objecting to that phrase because it *doesn't* recognize the meaning of the term?"

Fighter shouted, *Damnit, judge, don't stuff your brains inside your robe! Your feigned ignorance is plain as stains upon a mattress.*

Then freedom lawyer took control, whoaing warrior's horses as they raced along the fence.

"May it please the court, there is a second way to deal with this problem. I have D.C. precedent upholding a conviction for sol-pros based on the *context* of communication, including the non-verbal cues that we have here, without the need to pin down every spoken word."

I raised a photocopy of the case, walked it to the bailiff, who transported it to Bachover. I dropped another copy in Cardot's chubby hand.

Bachover glanced through the case, flipping pages as if shooing gnats. "This is doubtful, Mr. Campbell, since our case contains one word that *could* refer to lunacy, as in 'head case.' Or a psychiatric session, as in 'head shrink.' Or group leadership, as in 'head man'."

I paused to hear two voices shout inside my mind.

Warrior: *Judge, you'll refuse to see what's right before your eyes until you make me prove that fleas do fractions.*

Freedom lawyer: *Relax, it's vintage Bachover—sends you on a snipe hunt, helps a green defense attorney, and plays hero for a comely working girl.*

Warrior: *Judge, you're crazy as a tattered shirt! I like our courtroom banter, the challenges you toss, but—damnit!— here's a case that I should win!*

Freedom lawyer finally seized command, tamping my aggression with respect: "If it please the court, I have a third road that will lead to recognition of the term at hand. The government recalls its vice-squad officer to qualify him as an expert on the meaning of 'head job' in the District of Columbia."

Bachover showed surprise, then smiled as if confident he'd quickly stamp a dead-end on this avenue. "Very well. The court affords the government that opportunity."

Returning Welter Clapp to the witness chair, I repeated questions we'd rehearsed at recess. He answered every when, where, who, and what-context question I could think of to establish his awareness that there was a single meaning for "head job" in Washington, D.C.

When I paused to think of other ways to buttress this man's expertise, the judge snapped up the reins and cantered back along my road. He fired questions aimed to cripple the credentials of my cop. What happened next surprised us both.

Bachover scoffed, "Officer, have you heard those words used sexually in any place *except* the District of Columbia?

"Yes, indeed I have, your honor. When I was an M.P. with the Air Force, I must have heard that phrase two-thousand times. It meant the same thing in a dozen cities throughout southeast Asia and Pacific islands."

Consternation drew Bachover's lips into a horizontal slit. I leapt to my feet. "On the basis of this man's extensive knowledge, I move the court to recognize him as an expert on the meaning of the term 'head job'."

Bachover looked for help from Nathan Cardot. "Any cross-examination, counselor?" The student lawyer shook his head apologetically and returned to staring at his notes.

Nipsy Murray shifted and re-crossed her legs, looking mildly amused. *Does she see the humor in this concert of hypocrisy: two alpha males sparring over where she'll spend the night?*

"Your motion's granted, Mr. Campbell," sighed the judge.

Since Bachover had previously acknowledged the defendant had solicited *something* from the undercover officer, Clapp's revelation that head job meant fellatio came as an anti-climax.

Asserting we'd established all the elements of sol-pros, I announced, "The government now rests its case against Ms. Murray." I appended, "*Thank you,* Officer. You may step down from the witness chair."

"Mr. Campbell!" shouted Bachover, abruptly transformed to a tiger, his face ringed with rage.

What did I do this time? I let both hands fall to my sides, palms toward the bench, eyebrows raised to claim my innocence.

"Had there been a jury in this case I would have just declared a mistrial for the way your tone implied your *personal* endorsement of the witness' testimony!"

Fighter quipped, *Do I laugh now or wait til it gets funny?* Freedom lawyer shushed him: *Just be glad he didn't drop that brick of protocol through the bottom of your case.*

Our trial spiraled to its final act. Cardot made an automatic motion for acquittal based on insufficient evidence. The judge denied it instantly.

Cardot called no witnesses. If Murray testified in her defense she'd only pit her credibility against our stalwart officer, try to sell the judge some different version of their curbside chat.

What's more—or less—in his summation Cardot failed to erect a single theory of defense. Instead he stammered through the standard riff that doubt must lurk somewhere inside his client's oblique reference to fellatio. Bachover frowned at him and shook his head; I felt sorry for the kid.

Maybe he'd been told at Georgetown's legal clinic, "See if you can get this case assigned to Bachover. If there's a problem or a weakness in the prosecution's evidence, he'll pry it up. Just sit back and see what you can learn."

I rose for oral argument, centering my weight for what would be this trial's final struggle with the judge. Before I spoke a word, Bachover slammed his hammer on the bench and pronounced defendant guilty.

Warrior yelled, *Alright—we won!*

Bachover raised his brows at me: "Does counselor for the government have a recommended sentence?"

In these cases colleagues usually suggested lock-up time. Later they would wink paternally among themselves, "Looked like she could use a little pimp-free R & R."

I saw the chance to ply some freedom law and took a different tack. Drawing from a prosecutor's duty to do justice, first I mentioned the defendant's drug-possession background from her rap sheet in my file.

Next I proposed probation for Ms. Murray on condition she sign up for drug-rehab. I named a treatment program favored by the judge.

"The court was leaning in precisely that direction, Mr. Campbell. I'll order a probation officer to interview Ms. Murray and make sure that she's a worthy candidate."

So ended my first sol-pros trial, a tougher case than fighter forecast when defendant sashayed through the door. I was pleased to log another victory, moreso since our office usually lost non-jury cases tried before this gadfly to the government.

Now that it was over I was glad Bachover kept me on my toes and made me navigate his tough forensic maze. Moreover, freedom lawyer learned that he could harness fighter's discontent and find *solutions* to the task at hand.

Once more Horace L. Bachover won my admiration. Ultimately he followed legal rules instead of using his discretionary power to pervert proceedings to an outcome he desired. I hoped he sensed my personal regard for him along with mutual respect for freedom law.

Maybe all of that—plus Bachover's puckish sense of humor—was why he gave the U.S. government one entire day in court to prove the meaning of head job.

ME, PROCURING PROSTITUTES?

Most good lawyers live well, work hard, and die poor.
—Daniel Webster

Manstead Armstrong's puny frame belied his brawny name.
At five-feet-four he barely weighed one-hundred pounds.
When marshals book-ended him from jail, I thought they'd
lost their prisoner. He looked like he'd survived a
concentration camp for gnomes.

At his trial Armstrong wore the clothes he'd been arrested
in: torn slacks, checkered shirt, and grimy running shoes.
With three-days growth of dark black beard, he seemed
actively infectious.

Perhaps counsel for defense forgot to tell him he should
clean up for the court. Maybe other prisoners wouldn't let
him use the soap—he was probably so low on the food
chain he was floss for other inmates' meals.

Bart Seedfall was appointed to defend him on a single
charge: attempting to procure for prostitution purposes.
Sixty-something, Seedfall always bent his torso forward when
he stood or walked. His dentures clacked in protest when
asked to hold a vowel too long.

Judge Horace L. Bachover entered court, assumed the throne,
and banged his gavel as an exclamation point to the bailiff's
cry, "All rise!"

"Let's get started, gentlemen. I see Mr. Armstrong has signed
forms to try this case without a jury. Mr. Campbell, drop
your opening statement—call a witness for the government."

Clay Harrigan, vice-squad cop, sauntered to the witness chair.
In his middle thirties, he stood six feet tall inside a corduroy
sports coat and dark brown slacks.

With a sing-song voice he testified that at 8 p.m. three weeks
ago he'd seen Armstrong standing on a corner of Sixteenth

Street. Wearing ordinary street clothes, Harrigan approached him, said he'd just flown in from Houston, and was "looking for some action."

Knowing he'd arrived at the decisive moment of his narrative, Harrigan turned to face the judge. "The defendant —that's him in the courtroom in the blue shirt next to counsel for defense—stepped back and looked me up and down. Then he said, 'Give me fifty dollars and I'll put you with some ladies that will drive you wild'."

Locking eyes with Bachover, the officer continued, "Mr. Armstrong next described the various sex acts his girls. . ."

"Wait a moment, officer!" said the jurist, holding up his palm. "Do I hear objection from the counsel for defense?"

"Yes, your honor," stammered Seedfall, who'd been rustling pink-hued charging papers on his desk. Suddenly his face lit up. "There's been no evidence the would-be girls were his!"

Seedfall, my learned friend, you'd nap through a fire drill.

After a two-second pause the lawyer added, "... or that he *had* some girls... or even that the girls were *real!*" The last word sparked a smile from the judge, which spread to the bailiff, clerk, and even the defendant.

"Sustained as to the use of 'his'," declared the judge.

Harrigan named three types of sex that Armstrong said *the* girls could perform. "He told me how much each act cost. First, I had to hand him fifty bucks as earnest money. He said he'd put this in an envelope and apply it to his fee depending on what sex I chose. When I heard that, I identified myself as a law-enforcement officer and placed him under arrest."

Seedfall's cross-exam was brief and focused mainly on the point Judge Bachover had raised: "My client never showed you any girls, did he?"

"No, sir. That's why he's charged with *attempting* to procure."

Thanks, Harrigan, for that reminder to our judge.

Next I called the officer's associate in vice. He'd observed the conversation from a spot across the street. The cop backed up all his partner said except, of course, he couldn't hear the tête-à-tête.

Seedfall rose to cross-examine. "Officer, is it not true from where you stood you could see both sides of the block?"

A. Pretty much—apart from where a panel truck was parked.

Q. You never saw my client talk with any girls that night, did you?

A. No, sir.

Q. And you never saw any unescorted women on the block when your colleague and my client spoke?

A. No, sir. I did not.

What's he driving at? I wondered. *Surely he knows we've presented beaucoup evidence to convict his client of* attempt.

"No further questions," declared Seedfall, and resumed his seat.

"The United States rests." *God, I love saying that! Besides pumping up my ego, what an image it projects.*

Seedfall started cranking out a lengthy oral motion for a judgment of acquittal, a.k.a "M.J.O.A." I smiled to myself, recalling days of cigarettes when I had match books printed with those letters on the front. As counsel for defense, I'd hand one to a jurist at informal gatherings with the bench. "Just a reminder, judge, that the defense *never* rests."

Seedfall finished arguing. Pulling from my reverie, I grabbed our office file. A prudent colleague had tucked in a photocopy of D.C.'s major precedent on attempting to

88

procure. I scanned it til I found the holding: To defeat a motion for acquittal, the prosecution only needs to show "some evidence" that defendant's goal was to procure for sexual purposes.

I stood to cite the case and yoke it to my evidence but Bachover waved me off. "I needn't hear rejoinder from the government. Defendant's motion is denied. Mr. Seedfall, does your client wish to open a defense?"

I looked at Armstrong slumping in his chair like he was terminally depressed. "Defense calls the defendant," Seedfall said.

Armstrong slowly crossed the floor and clambered to the witness chair. He sat there for five seconds like an unmade bed. But his first words knocked me back. "Your honor, I confess that everything the officers just said was true."

More surprising was the verbal pigeon he next freed. In a whiney voice he said, "I'll admit that earlier I'd shot my final fix of heroin and was looking for some cash. But I'm a con man, judge, a Murphy Man. That's my only game. I stuff my mark's down-payment in an envelope, later switch it for one filled with paper, then I split."

He turned puppy eyes on Bachover and with in-your-pocket intimacy declared, "I've *never* had a string of girls. Look at me, your honor—no way a guy my size could be a pimp on Sixteenth Street. I'm just a penny-ante larcenist."

'Zounds, what a plausible defense! He's claiming no intent to furnish girls, just bag some easy cash. My case is coming off the rails. Now Seedfall can argue Armstrong can't be guilty of attempting to PROCURE because he's guilty of attempted LARCENY. We can't convict him of a crime we didn't charge!

Suddenly it struck me: Although I'm convinced he's guilty of attempting to procure, at heart he *is* a con man. And like all classic cons, his story vibrates with a tinny ring of truth.

Has my fighter once again misjudged the savvy of a Fifth Street lawyer? Maybe Seedfall's *not* a super-annuated nut one fall from being fossilized. He's yanked away my victory like a make-up artist snatches Kleenex from its box.

When he finished his narration Armstrong bowed his head and stared into his lap. Justice raised a pensive finger to her lips and silence reigned in court. Seedfall shuffled papers on his desk.

I'd watched Seedfall do this dance of documents before, buying seconds to decide what next to say. That was fine with me. I needed time to strategize my cross-exam. Since Armstrong said that his intent was *not* procuring sex, somehow I had to prove it *was.*

Should I attack his general credibility? Rules of evidence won't let me smack him with his lengthy rap sheet of arrests. But I could drill him with an actual conviction; his shoplifting certificate is stapled to my file. Or should I leave things as they are, not give him a chance to reinforce his con-man chronicle?

Seedfall looked up from his papers and declared, "Your honor, those are all the questions defense counsel has for Mr. Armstrong at this time."

Bachover peered down at me. "Mr. Campbell, does the government wish to cross-examine?"

My gut signaled Armstrong's story sounded too self-serving—too attached to his *con*-venient heroin *con*-fession. Despite Bachover's pro-defendant sympathies, the judge took pride in his street wisdom. He wouldn't want to think he could be fooled.

Does Bachover know that Armstrong pitched exactly the same con as the defendant in my photocopied case? In closing argument I'll make sure to cite that case and highlight that unusual coincidence.

"Mr. Campbell, the court is waiting."

I fingered through the papers in my file, using Seedfall's tactic to secure a moment more. Trials sometimes reach a point where lawyers have to make a crucial choice. I knew this was mine.

I went with my gut; it bet all our chips the judge would see through Armstrong's Murphy Man disguise.

So, for my first time as lawyer for the government, I waived the right to cross-examine a defendant. Instantly Seedfall followed with "Defense will rest."

Bachover seized command. "Mr. Campbell, I don't need your closing argument. I'll hear from the defense."

Oh, no! fighter thought. *Has the judge already thrown me from the train?*

Seedfall summarized our polar views of Armstrong's aims: procure sex or play a con? "It's up to you, your honor, to decide if you believe my client—or if his size and candidly confessed intent at least gives rise to reasonable doubt."

"I have no doubt at all," the judge declared and slammed his gavel on the bench. "This court finds Manstead Armstrong guilty as he's charged."

Right on, judge! Being an outspoken freedom jurist doesn't mean you have to be bamboozled by every pitiful defendant who spins a woeful tale. You'll still drop the hammer on a guy who tries to game the court.

Warrior was a wolfhound wagging double tails. But leaving court, instead of skipping down the hall, I only bumped my briefcase on one thigh in rhythm to the march "El Capitan."

As I hummed along, a mental finger toggled up my learning switch. *What if you tried a case like this before a jury? Would you impeach Armstrong with his shoplifting beef? Would you attempt to get his rap-sheet of arrests before the jurors once he put his character in evidence as a Murphy Man?*

Before a jury I'd do both! my fighter said. That notion sprung a basic insight from this case: Fundamental choices often rest on sizing up exactly who decides what's what.

Armstrong might have fooled some *jurors* into doubting his aim was procuring sex. And, as Clarence Darrow said of spawning doubt inside twelve jurors' minds, "All it takes is *one* to win for the *defense.*"

As my final duty of the day I dispatched an office memo. It warned how a Murphy Man defense could hobble allegations of attempting to procure. If they came across this kind of case at papering I urged them charge "in the alternative" attempted larceny.

If they caught a case like this on trial day, they should move the court to let them add the other crime. If defense cried, "Lack of notice" or "Unfair surprise!" they could always let the trial be postponed a couple days.

I argued this would be the counter to a phony con-man claim and also set the case up for a plea to one crime if we dropped the other.

My memorandum was received with office-wide indifference; nothing changed in papering or prosecution strategies at trial.

But that memo, the defendant, and yours truly had been yoked by karmic bonds. When I later left the office and returned to private practice, Manstead Armstrong would become my first appointed client, accused of the same crime.

When we met the second time, Armstrong said he didn't know if our reunion came about because the Blindfold Lady savored irony or had a wacky sense of humor. Likely it was both.

In our future trial a well-dressed, clean-shaved Armstrong took the witness chair and once again proclaimed his aim for petty-larceny.

But this time I handed him two envelopes so he could show the hocus-pocus switch of his mark's dollar bills for shredded paper cut to money size. In short, we chose a jury trial, played the con-man card again, and won.

92

CONVICTING AN INNOCENT MAN

No defendant is as scary as an innocent man.
—J. Michael Haller

One cold December evening in Washington, D.C., two sex-division cops banged on the door of Jason Dreme. When Dreme opened up, he stared into the barrel of a thirty-eight. Behind it was a forty-five.

Once inside, police arrested Dreme and his guest Cecil Camrock for the rape of Alice Fask. Cops let Camrock snag an army surplus jacket from Dreme's couch so he could wear it to the precinct. That coat was the fulcrum point of justice in this case.

Precinct cops conducted separate "interviews" with their two suspects and the victim. Eventually the officers decided there was insufficient evidence of rape to win at trial. The woman knew both guys, had invited them for sex, and then the scene turned rough.

However, when the cops routinely searched both men, they found a stolen credit card in Camrock's coat. They discovered Dreme had scribbled the cardholder's signature at different stores to buy a television, four mag wheels, and a bag of groceries.

A few days later two files, each with a cancelled count of rape, landed on my desk. What other charges should I lodge against these guys? Against Dreme I alleged three counts of forgery. I stuck his file in my desk and waited for a month to see if other forgeries would come to light.

I papered Cecil Camrock with receiving or possessing stolen property (R.S.P): the credit card. He had other charges pending: two burglaries and one assault, all allegedly on different dates, each slated for a separate trial.

Because police had focused on a charge of rape, the only fact supporting R.S.P. in their report was finding the pinched plastic inside Camrock's coat.

Among scores of cases I had papered, this was the only one for which I didn't write a tactical synopsis, making sure our evidence matched each element of crime. At the time it seemed a cinch; whoever tried this case would only have to show defendant knew his coat contained a stolen credit card.

Two months after Camrock's bust my boss directed me to try all cases sent Judge Waldo Witherspoon. As defense attorney I had argued motions half-a-dozen times before this introverted jurist. He was in his fifties, tall and gangly, smiling awkwardly when off the bench, tense and solemn in his robes.

At ten o'clock I climbed the gritty marble stairs to Witherspoon's domain. Five minutes later a policeman strolled inside and placed a file in my hand. "I'm Sergeant Palmer," he said, crunching my extended hand.

I recognized my scrawl along the folder's top: "U.S. v. Cecil Camrock." *First chance I've had to try a case I papered. What poetic justice—it's the only one I incompletely prepped!*

Palmer said, "This case was broken down from sexual assault but our rape victim thought she had to come to court. She's outside with my partner. Shall I let her go?"

Anything could leap out of a case I hadn't thoroughly prepared. "We just might need another witness. Ask your partner to escort her to my office and have her wait for me. I'll talk with her first time I get a chance."

"Oh," I added, "when you testify, don't tell the court you were investigating rape. That prejudicial fact could sock us with a mistrial."

"Right, I know the drill," Palmer replied. "We've also got the owner of that stolen credit card outside. He'll say when and where he lost the card and what its numbers are. Want to talk to him?"

"If I get time. First I'll see if Camrock's lawyer wants to cut a deal."

Ike Falton had just eased his seventy-year-old body through the door. Gaunt, with thinning hair, he wore a faded dark-blue suit and scuffed hush-puppy shoes. On close terms with mortality, apparently he'd parlayed for a shamble: partly shuffle, partly amble.

Ike was another Fifth Street lawyer, pleading truckloads of defendants guilty for each one he represented in a trial.

Despite my scorn for such attorneys—the way they milked the court-appointment system while they shoehorned clients into jail—since facing them in court I'd learned respect for their street savvy; they knew how to get inside a jury's mind.

Since we had three other cases against Camrock, I gave Falton time to grasp this ripe condition for a plea. He dropped into a chair and pulled out Camrock's papers from a dozen charging sheets he'd jammed between the pages of his bulging daily planner.

Approaching Falton's desk I said, "I'm surprised you haven't wrapped up Camrock's charges in a package deal."

"I would have, Campbell, but my guy insists he's innocent of R.S.P. At least I persuaded him to waive a jury trial. We should get this done by noon."

Camrock came to court in handcuffs with two gum-chewing marshals on his flanks. He was a handsome twenty-two-year-old, stocky in his Levis and a long-sleeved yellow shirt. The marshals clicked away his bracelets, then slouched against the courtroom wall one leap from their prisoner.

I turned toward the gallery and motioned to the owner of the stolen credit card. Before he could come forward, Witherspoon stepped into court to his bailiff's boom, "All rise! Please, be seated and..."

The judge cut short his introduction: "Let's get underway." The clerk intoned, "U.S. versus Cecil Camrock."

Witherspoon peered down at defendant and his counsel. "I understand that the accused has waived his right to jury and elected to be tried by me on one charge of receiving or possessing stolen property. Is that right, Mr. Camrock?"

"Yes, judge," said defendant with respect, still standing as his counselor dropped into a seat.

"Mr. Campbell, I don't need an opening statement. Let's hear from your witnesses."

I called the owner of the credit card. A businessman of middle age, he fidgeted between the fabric-polished arms of the courtroom's witness chair. Unrehearsed, his testimony wandered through a forest of irrelevance but there was no objection from defense.

Early last November he couldn't find his MasterCard and reported it as stolen to his bank. He recited its ten digits from a note he'd brought to court.

I handed him the credit card marked as government's Exhibit A; he said this was the one. Falton didn't even cross-examine.

I figured I'd need only one more witness: Sergeant Palmer, the arresting cop who'd found the stolen card in Camrock's coat. I turned to the officer. He rose from the front row of the gallery, took the oath, and settled in the witness seat.

I asked the routine opener: "Will you tell Judge Witherspoon the circumstances under which you first encountered Cecil Camrock?"

Falton struggled from his chair. "Objection!" he yelled, brandishing a crumpled charging sheet. "Campbell's getting into prejudicial matters that will ruin a fair trial!"

The judge raised his brows at me: "Mr. Campbell?"

"Your honor," I said, "both Sergeant Palmer and I know of the *potential* for some prejudice and we intend to keep it out of court."

"Very well," the jurist muttered in a guarded tone. He disliked making dicey calls on evidence. "With that assurance from the government, the witness may proceed."

Palmer testified that on the night in question Camrock "was at the precinct *on another matter* when I found a credit card inside the left front pocket of his coat."

I showed him government's Exhibit A. Yes, this was the card. Again no cross-exam by Falton. "Prosecution rests," I said.

Falton staggered to his feet: "I call my client to the stand."

Cecil Camrock only took three minutes to unwrap his wretched claim: The coat belonged to Jason Dreme. Camrock was just visiting the place where Dreme lived with a roommate "when two officers came in. They wanted me and Jason to go with them to the precinct. They let me grab Dreme's jacket off his couch when I said it was cold outside."

Camrock's tale came as no surprise: another version of *I didn't know the thing was loaded.* It seemed his only possible defense. Because the jacket wasn't his, he couldn't know the credit card inside was stolen—guilty knowledge being an essential element of R.S.P.

Although not allowed to mention this to Witherspoon, I noticed Camrock's words were chosen artfully. Not only did they craft a tough defense to penetrate, they shrewdly side-stepped every puddle that could splash his character with references to rape.

I felt a muffled rumble in my gut: *What if his account is true?* But as I rose to cross-exam, warrior kicked aside this thought. He was keen to slash at the defendant's story with his lie-detecting sword of truth.

Q. Mr. Camrock, will you please inform the court why Jason Dreme's not here to back your claim the coat was his?

A. I'm sorry, sir, I don't know where he is.

*That's because he's in the wind for forgery. You know
that too, you fox, but you're too smart to say it. And I
can't mention it without another source of prejudice
threatening your day in court.*

Q. Then can you tell us where Mr. Dreme's roommate is and
why he's not in court today to verify the coat belonged to
Mr. Dreme?

A. I asked him and I thought he'd come. I guess he didn't
show.

Feeling Camrock pinned against the ropes I aimed a parting
blow; not a power shot, just a jab to emphasize the lack of
any evidence to support his desperate claim.

Q. And what happened to that jacket the police returned
to you?

A. Uh, sir, I don't know.

"No further questions," I announced.

"Defense calls Officer Alonso Boomer," declared Falton,
shooting me a rictus grin.

*That's Sergeant Palmer's partner—what's he want this guy to
say? I didn't even need him for my case!*

Falton got permission from the judge to cross-examine
Boomer as a hostile witness, then challenged him to say the
jacket really was the property of Jason Dreme. "I don't
know *who* owned that jacket," was the cop's response.

Fallton smiled and turned to me. "Defense rests," he said.

I felt uneasy in my gut again. Boomer's statement barely
boosted Camrock's case but might cast doubt on mine. To
sweep away uncertainty, I recalled Sergeant Palmer.

With that act my karmic bill came due.

Routinely the policeman who transports our file to trial is the arresting cop. As if I hadn't heard the adage "a-s-s-u-m-e makes an ass of you and me," I assumed this when I first received our file-folder from the man.

I asked Palmer to describe precisely where the coat had been when he "invited" Camrock to the precinct that cold night. "Was it draped across Dreme's couch or did Mr. Camrock have it on already?"

Palmer stared at me in mild surprise. "I can't say, Mr. Campbell. I wasn't present when defendant left Dreme's place. That would be Officer Boomer." Quick as a slap, I realized I'd blown which cop was the arresting officer.

I stepped back and recalled Boomer to the stand. Even if he couldn't say who *owned* the coat, at least he should know if Camrock had been wearing it when he and Palmer first burst through the door, alert for any gun-concealing clothes.

But in answer to my question Boomer said, "I don't know *where* that jacket was or if defendant had it on when we came in."

Shee-ite—both cops now floodlighted what had been defense's tiny ray of doubt!

I retreated to my desk, seized our office file, and tore out the arrest report. "Officer Boomer," I asked, flourishing the document five feet from his face, "Would the P.D. form 163 *refresh your memory?*"

"Well, maybe," he replied, to my emphatic cue. I handed him the paper with my thumb pressed underneath one line.

"Do you see on your report where you wrote, 'Before he left, defendant asked if he could put on *his* coat'?"

I took two steps back, letting him peruse the form until he looked at me. "Did that refresh your memory, officer?" I asked, completing the required litany for non-impeachment questioning.

"Yes," Boomer said, "but I can't swear that it was his *own* coat."

My fighter felt a flash of fury at Boomer's emphasis. I toyed with dropping the entire charge. If this was the best these cops could do to prove their case of R.S.P., they shouldn't look for help from me!

But by the time the officer resumed his seat behind the rail, my fighter had reined in his rage. *I came to bury Cecil, not proclaim his innocence! I'll wrest a guilty verdict from this case regardless of two keystone cops.*

In summation for the judge I matched our evidence to every element of R.S.P. As for showing Camrock knew the credit card was stolen, I conceded "our case might at first seem weak, based, as proof of knowledge usually is, on circumstantial evidence."

"But," I added, "here it rests upon a solid law of human nature: In cold weather folks who visit someone's home wear coats. And when they leave they put them on again. Why *wouldn't* Mr. Camrock grab his own coat when he left?"

I went on, "Furthermore, two laws of truth-detection put the lie to Mr. Camrock's claim he didn't know the coat was loaded. First, it's too convenient, too hackneyed a cliché to be believed. Second, his self-serving story came with absolutely no corroboration. Where is Mr. Dreme, the would-be owner of the coat? Where is the roommate to back up this tale?"

As I sat down a strange thing happened. My fighter's racing pulse felt syncopated tapping from an inner ghost of doubt that Camrock actually was guilty of this crime. Once more my warrior shoved aside this infidel.

Witherspoon stared three seconds at the maple gavel resting on its side. Abruptly he looked up and cleared his throat. "I find Cecil Camrock guilty beyond reasonable doubt."

He grabbed his hammer, slammed it once against its wooden tray, and looked intently at the torpid U.S. marshals. They straightened up and started toward their detainee.

Then another weird thing happened, a disconcerting first in my career. As I glanced across the ten-foot chasm separating prosecutors from the people they accuse, I saw tears well up in Camrock's eyes.

Unnerved, I began replacing papers in our office file, treading time by filing each one chronologically. My mind flashed back to Camrock's testimony: It seemed so scrawny, stretched across my rack of cross-exam. Still, it may have been the truth.

When I looked up, the marshals had escorted Camrock from the room. I was relieved to see both cops had also disappeared. Not sure what I would have said to them, I knew I'd not have been a diplomat.

Walking to my office, I remembered Alice Fask, our would-be victim of a sexual assault. Would she still be waiting there? I found her pretzled in my desk chair, reading from a paperback, sipping coffee from a cardboard cup.

I introduced myself and announced the guilty verdict on our charge of R.S.P. She jumped from the chair, her initial grimace switching to a smile. "Thank God, you nailed Camrock's butt for *something!*"

"Right," I said, "but can you believe he claimed the stolen credit card was in *Dreme's* coat, that the army-surplus jacket wasn't his?"

She pressed her palms against her cheeks and gasped. "Oh no, what he said was true! Jason wore that coat when he and Cecil forced me to have sex with them. Cecil didn't bring a coat that night."

I felt trapped inside a falling elevator. *Great Scot, my worst prosecution nightmare—I've convicted someone who was innocent!*

* * * * *

After what seemed hours plummeting in freefall—it was less than seven seconds—I caught my breath and felt my feet

rest on the floor. I forced a casual tone and thanked Fask
for her candor. I said I'd have to set the record straight
about that jacket and the credit card.

"He's got other charges on him, right? So he won't be
making bail? I don't want him coming after me."

I confirmed the other pending trials, the small chance
Camrock's residence would change from a Club Fed address.
Pushing through a storm of doubt, I walked my career's
most potent un-called witness to the door.

When she left I dropped into my office chair.

What were my obligations, options, and their consequences?
Can my law-trained mind unscramble logic from this perfect
storm of thoughts?

After five heart-racing minutes freedom lawyer calmed me
down and tendered his report. Fask's statement linked me
to three rings of duty: the Constitution, legal ethics, and
morality. Each required that I right the wrong I'd caused.

I lurched from my chair, snatched our office file, and marched
down the hall. Time to trigger option one. I rapped on
Clovis Bankwood's door.

Summarizing Camrock's trial, I concluded with my post-
verdict surprise. "When you think about it, boss, why would
anyone in his right mind grab a jacket that he knew
contained a stolen credit card and take it to the precinct
where he knew that he'd be searched?"

I argued we must now reopen and dismiss his charge of
R.S.P. I added, "Boss, here's a chance to do what's right *and*
show D.C. residents we're as keen for justice as we are to
throw folks in the slammer. If our office could project that
public image, wouldn't jurors be more likely to believe us
next time we claim, 'Hey, *this* guy is guilty'?"

Bankwood didn't say a word, just pointed toward the file in
my hand. I spread it open on his desk. He scanned the rape-

case portion and then paused at Camrock's list of pending charges. "Here's your trouble, Art—sometimes you *think* too much. Camrock's not an Eagle Scout. He's the reason we're both prosecutors."

"That's true, boss, but the fact remains he's innocent of R.S.P. At the very least we've got a constitutional duty to disclose exculpatory evidence to defense."

"Don't sweat it, Art," Bankwood said dismissively. "We've got so much on Camrock, he'll go away for years. One R.S.P. will hardly make a difference." He leaned back in his chair, his wintry stare implying our debate was done.

Feeling rib-kicked, I retrieved the file and trudged back to my office. Did Sophocles include U.S. attorneys when he said, "No one has more sacred obligations to obey the law than those who make the law?" We'd just made the law for Cecil Camrock.

Freedom lawyer felt provoked. *Bankwood didn't order me to do one thing or another. He only said "don't sweat" this case. Time to activate my second plan.*

I phoned Camrock's lawyer and related how I'd stumbled onto evidence that proved his client's innocence. His reaction caught me short.

"Campbell, don't you lay that trip on me! If these facts come out, Camrock can sue me for not interviewing Fask and calling her for the defense. You've got your conviction, Art. Now leave me alone."

I hung up the phone in shock. Was I a Pollyanna, thinking there was more to litigation than just hacking without caring where the pieces fell? I'd just witnessed both sides of our adversary system say they would ignore their duties under legal ethics and the Constitution.

I never had insisted other lawyers practice freedom law; that was *my* career-choice. But was I a starry-eyed idealist to feel disgust when I observed due process skewered by the very men we trust to make it work?

Picking up the phone again, I called the courtroom of Judge Witherspoon. The clerk said he was in his office waiting my return, so we could start another trial.

I walked to the jurist's chambers. Witherspoon was sitting in his robes behind a desk of open files, eye-glasses thumbed up into wavy chestnut hair. I told him of my just-discovered fact. From this decisive evidence Camrock was not guilty. Would the judge declare a mistrial in this case?

His features clouded with concern. "I'm sorry, Mr. Campbell, but this is not my problem. It's Clovis Bankwood's or Camrock's attorney. Today you convinced me of defendant's guilt. Tomorrow I don't want to see myself lambasted in the POST for being so dim-witted or pro-government I didn't even find a reasonable doubt in Camrock's case."

I was stunned. This time Herman Melville's censure leapt to mind: "Who's to doom when the judge himself is dragged before the bar?"

Three separate mandates ordered me to right the wrong done here. I'd come up with three solutions, placing them before three men. Each side-stepped his duty to an innocent accused.

Exiting the judge's chambers, I walked to his courtroom, sat down at my desk, and pondered my next move.

When Witherspoon resumed the bench to start another trial, I asked the courtroom clerk to recall Camrock's case. He started pawing through a pile of files.

Not wanting to surrender my momentum, I handed him our office file, so he could introduce it for the court reporter. I wanted an official record of what would happen next.

"A matter in United States versus Cecil Camrock on the charge of R.S.P. Mr. Campbell is appearing for the government. Neither the defendant nor his counsel is before the court."

"What's going on here, Mr. Campbell?" scowled Judge Witherspoon.

"Counsel for the government requests the court reopen this proceeding because he's come across significant new evidence."

Witherspoon sighed, "Very well. Motion to reopen granted, Mr. Campbell. Anything else you'd like to do before we get on with our work today?"

"Yes, your honor, one more thing." *Hang on, you old trout, or hang it up!* "Counsel for the government now enters a nolle prosequi in this case."

"What—you refuse to prosecute—you're dropping the R.S.P. charge?!"

"That's correct, your honor. Post-trial evidence I discovered corroborates Mr. Camrock's defense, in effect exonerating him. Not only does the Constitution require that I make this known to the defense—I have—but professional responsibility and the interests of justice dictate this disposition of the case."

"Okay, Mr. Campbell," sighed the judge. "I hope you know what you are doing. The charge of R.S.P. against Cecil Camrock is dismissed. Mr. Clerk, please call the calendaring court and have it send another trial we can start this afternoon. I'll be in my chambers til it comes."

* * * * *

Sitting at my table waiting for a new case to arrive, I felt my pulse rate slowly throttle back. I thought about the consequences of my acts. What reprisals lay in store?

I'd upset a defense counsel and a judge. No big problem there; I did that every day. But what about my boss? Would I be fired or demoted when word got back to Clovis Bankwood?

Of one thing I felt absolutely sure: I'd reached the right result in Camrock's case. He might well be guilty of some other crimes—and if so, we'd nail him. But the guy was clearly innocent of R.S.P.

I looked back at my education as a prosecutor. I'd learned much from those for whom I first had minimal respect. My teaching corps included wily Fifth Street lawyers, volcanic judges, and over-zealous colleagues.

But not until today had all three stiff-armed my belief that our Blindfold Lady always tried to stumble forward to a self-correcting stance.

A shudder rippled through my staunch faith in our adversary system. Due process failed when its key participants ignored their designated roles.

Yes, that was it. Camrock's case had been a threat to more than my belief in freedom law. My forcing its finalé seemed essential to uphold the rule of law itself.

I'd need more time to process all the implications of this case: legal, moral, and vocational. Right now I had to put them all on hold; another trial just marched through the courtroom door.

ROUGH & TUMBLE JUSTICE

*It's not how hard you hit. It's how hard you get hit—
and keep moving forward.—Rocky Balboa*

Moments after unconvicting a defendant who was innocent,
I began another case. Although the facts were simple, it
turned out to be my toughest trial as a prosecutor.

One mid-December afternoon on Fifteenth Street, Jorge
Croze climbed in the backseat of a taxicab. The cab, driven
by Elijah Caveson, made its way to Eighteenth Street and
paused before a traffic light. Suddenly Croze lurched
forward, slammed his fist into the driver's jaw, then twice
more in his upper cheek.

A policeman, strolling only forty yards away, heard a cry for
help, saw the cabby's bloody face, and arrested Croze. The
defendant's motive—robbery, race, or politics—never shook
loose from the case.

Two other witnesses had eye-balled the scene. One was a
thirty-year-old architect who'd stepped off a curb to hail the
cab. The other was a middle-aged pedestrian poised to cross
the intersection from the other side. Each stood less than ten
yards from the scene.

From a prosecutor's view, the trial should have been an easy
one-round knockout. But forensic gremlins changed it to an
eight-round, take-no-prisoners bout that dragged on for three
sweat-stained days.

When the arresting officer handed me our office file, one
gremlin grinned from names on its front page: In defendant's
corner crouched a legendary pettifogger, attorney Harry
Blockburn.

Apparently Blockburn had tried this case last month against
another prosecutor and secured a draw. The cryptic entry
on our file stated, "Judge granted the defendant's motion for
a mistrial on day five."

How did Blockburn stretch this simple case of battery to five entire days?

The courtroom door banged open and in marched the man himself. Aged forty-plus, Blockburn wore a checkered coat that strained against the single button on its front. A nest of flaxen ringlets settled on his five-foot-ten-inch frame.

His greeting—"Hi, kid, think you'll go the distance?—telegraphed his pugilistic style. I stared at his ample paunch and said, "Looks like you need a little roadwork, Hal." He brushed aside my counter-shot as if he hadn't heard.

Behind his lawyer walked defendant Croze. He was Blockburn's age and height, minus thirty pounds. Cuban-born, he wore a tailored blue-serge suit; his chiseled features could have graced the pages of a male fashion magazine.

Blockburn's secret weapon—known to all who ever sat or stood beside him—was his shunning of deodorants. I tried to keep to a strategic distance. But bench conferences, especially by afternoon, were like tête-à-têtes in an abandoned abattoir.

Round One: Waiting for Judge Witherspoon and jurors to arrive, I chatted with the clerk whose desk adjoined the judge's bench. My opponent stood hip-shot next to Croze behind defendant's table.

Abruptly Blockburn grabbed his client by an elbow. Steering him across the courtroom to the prosecutor's desk, he pushed him down into my chair.

"What's going on, Blockburn?" I said, striding towards his client til I stood above him. "Mr. Croze, you'll have to move out of my seat."

"No way, Campbell!" Blockburn said and pressed down on his client's shoulders. As I stepped back from the lawyer's potent fumes, he rolled up on me: "It's not fair that counsel for the government sits closer to the jury box than the

108

defense. Makes it look like the defendant is an outcast while jurors and the prosecutor are on one side against him."

Caught flat-footed, all I could do was slide my papers to the table's other end. I refused to yield the entire space, and mused, *Nice shot, Blockburn. I've often thought this seating favors prosecution points of view. But do you really want to spar with me on this? Just wait for my next move.*

"All rise!" the bailiff ordered and Judge Waldo Witherspoon strode into court. As Croze stood, I walked behind him, gripped the armrest of "my" chair, and pulled it next to me. When the bailiff chanted, "Please, be seated," I obeyed. *Let Witherspoon decide where Croze will sit.*

"Your honor!" blustered Blockburn. "Counsel for the government just swiped my client's chair!"

Witherspoon replied, "Take it easy, Mr. Blockburn. That's the prosecution's customary place. You've tried sufficient cases in this courtroom to know that."

But the lathered lawyer made a formal motion to reverse the standard seating plan, repeating for the record what he'd just rehearsed with me.

Clearly disinclined to start this trial ruling who should win a game of musical chairs, Witherspoon asked, "Would the government mind swapping tables with defense for this one case?"

"We'd be glad to if your honor orders it," I said obligingly. *Sorry, Judge, I won't let you off the hook of having to decide. That's your job. If Croze appeals, I won't waive our right to brief this point and finally settle it with law.*

"So ordered, Mr. Campbell," muttered Witherspoon, looking downcast like he'd just found too much hair twined in his comb.

At least he's not spewing fury because twenty minutes earlier I'd set free a man he'd said was guilty. I shoved papers in my briefcase and moved to the other desk.

Round Two: Half a minute before our juror candidates were slated to arrive, Blockburn stood and made an oral motion "to strike the entire jury panel. I'm sure it won't consist of native Spanish-speakers, people in their forties, or my client's race. So defendant will not have a jury of his peers."

His move hit me like a head-butt on my chin. *Karma strikes again! He just paraphrased the motion Lois Goodman filed months ago when I was her co-counsel for defense. He's free-wheeling complex issues that took two weeks for me to trounce as prosecutor in Judge Bachover's court.*

Blockburn shuffled on: "I observe—and let the court correct our record if I'm wrong—that my client and his witnesses are white." He turned and gestured to three well-dressed men sitting in the front row of the gallery. They nodded to the judge.

"By contrast," he continued, "except for the arresting officer, all three prosecution witnesses are black." Surprise skipped across the judge's face at what seemed a blatant racist argument.

"Your honor," I responded, "the proper demographic of a jury is pending resolution in both the U.S. and the D.C. Court of Appeals. If a ruling comes down in his favor, Mr. Blockburn has preserved this issue for his client. So for the record the government opposes the defense request."

"Defendant's motion is denied," said Witherspoon in an uncertain tone. He was not a man who reveled in command; now he was distinctly ill at ease. Before a single witness had been sworn, he'd had to make two oral rulings on two novel points of law. Each decision could be subject to appellate scrutiny.

At least I spared us all a lengthy hearing on that motion. But Blockburn's strategy was starting to emerge: throw every punch conceivable, any place, at any time.

After jurors were selected—mercifully with only minor Blockburn clinches—Witherspoon declared recess for the day.

110

<u>Round Three</u>: Back in court at 10 a.m., my opening statement sketched for jurors what our evidence would show. Then our four witnesses testified, filling in my sketch with neatly overlapping details. Each added sound and color to a five-second scene of what appeared to be an unprovoked attack by the defendant Croze.

Except for the cabby, Blockburn merely threw light jabs at our witnesses. His cross-examination stressed their distance from the incident and implied they never had the chance to see the "driver actually start the fight."

But he opened with a knock-out punch against our man who drove the cab. "Mr. Caveson, isn't it a fact you've slanted all your testimony here because last week you slapped a $20,000 lawsuit on my client?"

I grit my teeth but couldn't block this blow. It was a valid shot to show potential witness bias. *Damn, I wish someone had told me this before the trial! I would have brought it out myself to prove I wasn't hiding anything.*

The lawsuit was, of course, the major gremlin in our trial, escalating it into a knock-down-drag-out bout. If Blockburn could destroy or weaken our cab-driver's testimony—even better, win this case—he'd gain leverage to negotiate or terminate the civil suit.

But even with no prepping on this point, our cabby deftly parried the attorney's punch. A veteran of D.C. muggings, he looked Blockburn in the eye and calmly stated, "No, sir, I am simply saying what your client did to me."

With low-keyed dignity Caveson next warded off Blockburn's fusillade of red-faced accusations that it was he who somehow twisted in his driver's seat and threw the first punch at his fare. Unable to spark anger in the witness, Blockburn finally dropped his arms, and stalked back to his chair.

<u>Round Four</u>: Judge Witherspoon announced our luncheon recess. I noticed Caveson head toward the witness room

where I had placed his wife to wait until she testified. At the door he asked her for a cigarette.

Then I spotted Blockburn trailing Caveson. When he spied the cigarette exchange, the lawyer bellowed for a U.S. marshal: "Officer, come quick and watch these prosecution witnesses—they're comparing testimony!"

Ninety minutes later Witherspoon reconvened our trial. But not until the final juror took her seat did Blockburn leap from his. "Your honor, something urgent has come up. Can we discuss it at the bench?"

Fragrant as a summer dumpster, he insisted we conduct a full-blown hearing to determine what transpired just outside the witness room. Caveson had seemingly defied the judge's standing order: Witnesses could not confer until they all had testifyied.

Freedom lawyer halted Blockburn's high speed wind-mill by pledging not to summon Mrs. Caveson as witness for the prosecution. I had saved her for rebuttal only if the jury needed a description of her husband's swollen face two hours after the attack. Since Croze's punches hadn't been disputed, I wouldn't need her testimony.

However, in his later jury argument, Blockburn twisted my concession into a low blow for the defense. He urged our jurors to draw adverse inferences from the spouse's non-appearance as a witness. "The D.A. is a good lawyer. He introduced her to you on voir dire. Let him tell you why he didn't put her on the stand."

Blockburn knew I could not respond without breaching protocol that counsel can't refer to facts the jury hadn't seen or heard. I couldn't mention how Blockburn had tried to kindle a bummed cigarette into a lengthy side-bar hearing, how I'd spared us all that waste of time. Now if I stepped into his concealed uppercut he'd score an instant victory, a.k.a. mistrial.

Was this the way he stopped the prior trial—buffeting the prosecutor with cheap shots until my colleague made a fatal slip in Blockburn's puppy-yuk? He sure knew how to pummel someone's bother-buttons.

Arms pinned at my side, feeling helpless to retaliate against his potent blow, I arose, my mind groping for some countermove.

In light of Blockburn's jury-poisoning words, I'll tell the judge that fairness should entitle me to reopen prosecution's case and put our "missing witness" on the stand.

Witherspoon snagged my gaze, half-closed his eyes, and slowly shook his head. I caught his message and sat down, seething secretly. This trial was being sucked inside the whale of a prosecutor's nemesis, the beast called Reasonable Doubt.

Round Five: Before describing Blockburn's next erratic bob-and-weave, I need to summarize a point of law.

After every prosecution witness testifies, defense has the right to scrutinize all written statements this person gave the government about the case. If a given statement can't be found, it's presumed to hurt the prosecution's side. That's to make sure we don't benefit from "accidentally losing" undesirable statements. If we can't find a missing document, the judge must strike all testimony of that witness.

In this trial every time I finished direct examination of a witness I thought, *No doubt Blockburn will invoke the rule and try to strike the testimony. And if he gets a single person's words thrown out, he'll next move for a mistrial. He'll argue jurors' minds have been incurably corrupted by the stricken testimony; they can't erase it from their memories; a bell can't be unrung.*

Blockburn didn't let me down. After each direct he insisted he be given every statement by that witness. His demands took place at bench conferences which by this time sorely taxed my nostrils. (Our court reporter backed her tripod to the far end of the bench.) Each time I thwarted his attack by handing over photocopies of all statements from that witness in my file.

On the second day of trial Blockburn waited til our jurors settled in their seats. Then he asked for still another conference at the bench to garner written statements. He claimed more reports existed than I'd furnished him.

But by that time I had done some homework. For the record and his honor, I disclosed what I had learned from talking to my colleague who had tried this case before.

In that trial Blockburn halted the proceedings and insisted on a special hearing about prior statements. With subpoenas he had summoned five policemen to tell the judge what witness information they had written down. Each one swore there were no other statements than the ones inside our file.

Today more copies of these documents were precisely what I'd placed in Blockburn's hand.

"Is that true, Mr. Blockburn?" inquired the judge accusatorily.

"Well, . . . yes, your honor. . . . But at that trial both the architect and the pedestrian testified they'd signed *another* statement for the government. . ."

"Therefore," I interrupted, "from that trial my learned colleague knows those so-called statements merely verified each witness' name and street address."

"Mr. Blockburn, is that also true?" asked Witherspoon, now clearly piqued.

"Uh. . . yes," he mumbled, staring at the judge's napping gavel. "But in my client's interests I needed to be sure that nothing's changed since then."

"Counsel, take your seats," commanded Witherspoon. Fighter tossed his foe a silent parting epithet: *Blockburn, you'd*

complain if you were hanged with unclean rope—until then
you stamp around this courtroom like you're banned from hell.

<u>Round Six</u>: To launch his case for the defense, Blockburn
called his client to the witness chair.

Croze spoke with the strained refinement of self-taught
elocution. As expected, his defense was that the cabby struck
him first. He claimed Caveson had turned his torso in the
driver's seat and, without a word or warning, simply started
hitting him. "No, he didn't leave a mark, and I have no idea
why he did it. I simply tried to stop him with my fists."

Croze then testified at length about his stature as a civic
leader in his neighborhood. I remembered from his opening
statement, Blockburn promised he would call three witnesses
to show his client's "outstanding moral character."

I welcomed this defense. It permitted me to contradict the
claim with more than certified *convictions* of defendant's
prior crimes. I could now impeach his client's reputation
with all the crimes for which he'd merely been *arrested*.

I stood up to cross-examine, clutching Croze's lengthy rap
sheet. Blockburn raised his chin and beckoned me. I came
close enough for him to whisper, "You'd better tender me a
copy." Although I planned to do this after I had cross-
examined Croze, I didn't mind affording him a little extra
time. I offered him a photocopy from my file.

He refused to take the paper from my hand! I dropped it
back on prosecution's desk. Abruptly, Blockburn leaned his
heavy torso toward me. Loud enough to reach the ears of
front-row jurors, he exclaimed, "May I have a copy of what
you are about to use?"

This time I ignored him and continued walking toward the
witness chair. "So that's the way you want to play this game!"
he muttered once again within the jury's range.

On cross-exam I didn't ask Croze anything about the
punching incident. I wouldn't let him reinforce his version

115

with more self-serving details or denials. Instead, like tugging out reluctant teeth, I got him to admit to each of five arrests.

The first three busts were for disorderly conduct, drunk driving, and too loud a party after ten p.m.

The final two were for battering victims with his fists. When I finished with the time and place of these arrests, I shot the jury a knowing glance. Seeing not a single frown of censure for my tactic, I decided to sit down.

Blockburn waisely didn't use his other witnesses. He knew I'd ask each one about their friend's arrests.

Round Seven: Seasoned boxers know how quickly they can blow a fight by not remaining wary near the end. I recalled this on the third day of our punch-and-parry contest.

It came time for both of us to argue to the jury. From defendant's corner Blockburn slowly rose and recounted his best shots. He emphasized the $20,000 suit against his client, how this made our cabby's version so self-serving it was worthless in the jurors' search for truth.

Although I felt this as a body-blow, it was proper argument. Then Blockburn stooped and looped another shot below my belt.

"My client was a freedom fighter, forced to flee his native land. Now he's being sued by Mr. Caveson—and the U.S. government has volunteered to act as Caveson's collection agency!"

"Objection!" I responded, springing from my chair. "Sustained," replied a tired and exasperated judge.

When it came my turn to argue, I got up swiftly like a last-round fighter seeking to secure a few more points. Even freedom lawyer was determined to deflate this bluster bag.

But I dropped my guard by letting slip a fact that wasn't in the evidence. In response to Blockburn's prior punch below my belt, I said, "Ladies and gentlemen, far from coming here to boost his civil suit, Mr. Caveson came to court three days ago for what he thought would be defendant's sentencing."

No matter that this fact was absolutely true—the cabby hadn't known his prior trial had misfired—there was not one whisper from the witness stand to back up my assertion; plus my words implied that Croze had been convicted in a prior trial.

Blockburn sprang out of his chair: "Defense strenuously objects and moves for a mistrial in this case!"

Oh no! He's knocked me off my pins in closing argument—after I've stayed cool for three whole days!

"Denied," ruled Witherspoon. Then he casually appended, "Mr. Campbell, please don't argue facts that aren't in evidence."

Saved by a judge as weary as I am of Blockburn's sand-box lawyering!

(As things turned out this error was defense's major focus on appeal—which shows how little merit Blockburn's other points contained. Months later his appeal was denied, my remarks dismissed as "harmless error... mistaken words cast in the heat of battle.")

Having barely ducked this late-round T.K.O., I decided I would follow the advice Judge Bachover once passed on to me. I understated my position, banished every hint of sarcasm, argued in my calmest voice. Fighter thus compressed all his accumulated wrath and let its power thud home inside neutral verbal gloves.

Our jurors spent two hours in their private room. When they returned, their forewoman placed her palms upon the wooden rail. Staring boldly into Croze's eyes, she pronounced him guilty.

Yes! My right hand tingled like it just had dealt the knock-out blow.

Round Eight: Flares of fisticuffs with Blockburn's blabber-worm were not complete. As soon as our last juror straggled from the courtroom, counsel for defense asked Witherspoon for instant sentencing. He waived his client's right to have a sentence based on background data to be gathered in a court report.

Good move, Blockburn! That report would bring to light two more arrests for Croze than I had used against his "law-abiding character." What other adverse information lurked inside our State Department files?

To get this data spread before the court, I toyed with raising what would be another novel issue: "The government should also have the right to a fair sentence, based on all the facts."

But freedom lawyer cautioned, *Not in a misdemeanor case, especially where you can't cite specifics that the judge should know.* So I gave Croze the benefit of silence on this point.

Still, warrior was itching to respond. So I said, "Your honor, as you contemplate a sentence, I'll just paraphrase attorney Blockburn's words before the jury and request that Mr. Croze not suffer for any untoward actions of his lawyer."

Already on his feet, Blockburn leapt into a two-step of lividity. "Now I know why the government has pursued my client through two long trials—it's to get back at me!"

Warrior thought, *"Harry Blockburn, you're as nutty as a sweater full of squirrels!"*

With long-suffering tones Witherspoon rebuked me for "unnecessary mockery." But his clerk, our bailiff—even our reporter—nodded their approval to me for the blow I'd struck on their behalf.

The judge imposed a six-month sentence, half in jail, the balance on probation. It seemed a fitting climax to three punches in a taxicab and three days of slugging in a court.

FINAL MOVE

Lack of due process is not an option.
—Judge Norbert Ehrenfreund

The cosmos does not ask us to be
perfect, only authentic. —AWC

I'd just won a guilty verdict after three combative days. But far from tired elation, I felt strangely ill at ease. Instead of striding from the courtroom with a victor's gait, I trudged slowly to my office, turned inside, and locked the door.

Why do I suddenly feel uncomfortable wearing prosecutor shoes?

Dropping in my chair, I raised my heels and propped them on the D.C. Code. I needed to reflect upon my last few days in court—especially the case that ended fifteen minutes before my last trial had begun.

I thought about the armload of misgivings I'd carried to the office on my first days as prosecutor. But most dissolved in papering when I was given full discretion whom to charge and with what crimes.

Since then, both in and out of court, my freedom lawyer never shivered helping scores of guilty people find new lodgings in D.C.'s cross-bar hotel.

So why are old uncertainties cropping up again? They began to surface midway through the trial of a stolen credit card: U. S. versus Cecil Camrock. That's where I convicted a defendant who was innocent.

No one in my office had admonished me about my later act of unconvicting him. Since three days had passed with no word from on high, I figured I would not be fired. But I had crossed the clear intention of my boss and that would bring some consequence.

119

*Yes, that case is where the acid drip onto your confidence
began. Why don't you retrace your steps to see if you can
find what this is all about?*

Images began to cyclone through my mind like pieces of a
jigsaw puzzle. But missing sections kept them from
condensing into something comprehensible.

I looked at the initial guilty verdict in the Camrock case. I
shouldn't be upset at that. Some folks are simply innocent.
When I'd tumbled onto this and got his charges dropped, the
scales of justice regained equilibrium.

Nor should I be shocked a thing like that could happen.
From the time I started trying cases, I knew each one had
its weaknesses.

Indeed, my education as a freedom lawyer came from
searching out a case's weakest links. Sometimes duty called
me to attack these links, other times to shield them from
attack or forge a stronger chain.

*Perhaps it's time to re-examine your professional beliefs and
if they've changed since you became a prosecutor.*

There's no question I've encountered more defects in the
trial process. But these were caused by flawed participants,
human errors, not short-circuits in the courthouse board.

From time to time I've heard cops and others "testi-lie."
Distorted specters also stalked through courtrooms, released
by biased witnesses or ones using strict economies of truth.

Even would-be honest witnesses often relied on imagination
more than memory. Sometimes judges only recognized a
law or fact that fit their private codes or mental frames.

But other aspects of our system—fact investigation, legal
research, cross-examination, or appeal—typically stepped in
and straightened out the bottom line.

120

Indeed, regardless if I won or lost, all my trials as a prosecutor reinforced my faith that, as a way of separating truth from rubbish, flack, and lies, the adversary *system* has no equal on this earth.

Since I became a lawyer for the government, I've visualized due-process as a triangle: prosecution, defense, and a judge. If one side goes slack, the others hold the form intact. Even when three sides wobble, the system keeps its shape enough to function in a world of less-than-perfect players.

So, I've learned a lot about participants and the way the law game's played but nothing's torn my faith in law itself.

Then what aspect of U.S. versus Camrock keeps jabbing in your ribs?

I pictured the defendant's street-wise face. By refusing to plea-bargain on a bogus charge of stolen property, he trusted he would be acquitted—and wept when Lady Justice let him down.

I replayed scenes from his trial's aftermath: confrontations with my boss, defendant's counsel, and the judge: how each had failed to function in his role.

But in that case defense's scales were also graced with unaccustomed weight. First was the testimony of two straight-talking cops. Both passed up the chance to nudge their suspect into jail; instead their words surprisingly sparked doubt about his guilt.

Add to this one crucial revelation from the victim of defendant's sexual attack. Badly wanting him in jail, she could easily have stood mute when I told her of the case's mystery coat.

Instead her candid exclamation handed me defendant's freedom key; I merely turned it in his cell. This evidence was what had finally made Dame Justice step back and reweigh her scales.

But Camrock's tear-glazed face still haunts me. What is it about his case?

I flashbacked to my boyhood when I sometimes choked back tears as victim of a railroad job. My domineering father never ceased competing with his son, sometimes like a playground bully, sometimes changing rules so he would always win. "It won't kill him, only make him stronger," was his rationale.

No wonder you became a boxer and a trial lawyer—by proxy you're still fighting battles lost in childhood.

Abruptly a new puzzle piece dropped in place. When I'd unleashed my warrior's will to win on Camrock Camrock, I'd done to him what my dad did to me!

This thought thudded like cement inside my gut. To check if it was true, I replayed my moves in Camrock's trial. Again I felt my fighter's lust for victory fuse with anger over non-supportive cops.

Yes, I'd bullied the defendant in the witness chair, convincing first myself and then the judge of Camrock's guilt. I'd railroaded him to jail.

My conscience leapt to my defense: "But when all was said and done, didn't freedom lawyer make things come out right?"

That's true, of course, but something still feels wrong....
Camrock's case still gnaws my self-assurance. It's something more than fighter's all-out will to win. That discovery is serious but it hasn't made me sleep so fitfully the last two nights.

I sensed Camrock's spirit prodding me to look again at the concluding segments of his case. Suddenly I slung my heels off the D.C. Code.

Now you've got it—they all fit!

I stared at what was finally a coherent picture. Seen on a deeper level, those post-trial scenes did not just show my boss, defense attorney, and a judge stumble in their roles.

These men did more than merely botch their obligations as sworn officers of law. Each steadfastly had *refused* to act. Their determined abdication—each for his own reason—was what injected toxin in my spirit as a prosecutor.

I reflected on the actions of my boss. When a prosecutor plays by Machiavelli's rules and neither judge nor counsel for defense resists, our system and all hope for justice is destroyed.

That brought to mind another lawyer's warning: "Ends justify the means in court only if the legal system is a fraud."

Clovis Bankwood's let-him-rot approach would transform law to a commodity, procured from prosecutors in return for get-tough reputations or delusions of self-righteousness.

Ike Falton, the attorney for defense, would trade a client's innocence to cover up exposure of his own ineptitude. Judge Waldo Witherspoon would leave a blameless man in jail so he could duck embarrassment.

I remembered how I'd teased defense attorneys about prosecutors' roles as stewards of the people's trust: "If all prosecutors played fair, our system wouldn't really need a lawyer for defense." Now I saw how twisted was the *premise* of my quip.

Time to cast these insights on the screen of your commitment to the law. Can your call to freedom law still function in their light?

First, to practice freedom law *effectively,* I must pare away illusions. Indeed, nearly every case that's come into my hands has been—to large or small degree—an exercise in *dis*-illusionment.

Camrock's was a case in point. My discoveries of today first had to break through my attachment to *ideal* roles—for judges, prosecutors, and defense attorneys—my personal investment in how key players were *supposed* to act.

Damn! Despite your constant vow to practice in the real world, part of you has still been living in the realm of fantasy—where purely good fights purely bad, and only right makes might.

Once more I heard echoes of Cut Cummings and my wife. Both had cautioned me against my penchance for "idealistic arrogance." I winced; it hurt to scrape so near the bone.

What if you dig so deep there's not enough to hold you up?

Okay, it's safe to start with metaphors. Time to put aside my icon of due process as a self-correcting triangle of prosecutor, counsel for defense, and judge. That image simply isn't accurate.

More realistic was the symbol I employed in pre-prosecutor days: The adversary system is a time-worn hawser pulled by the defense and prosecution in a robust tug of war.

Now, Campbell, do you dare project these insights on your future as a lawyer for the government?

I squinted down the corridor of a career in Washington, D.C. What emerged were shadows from a set of doors I hadn't seen before.

Behind them sat politicoes who—regardless of the rationales they sold the press and sometimes bought themselves— would use their power to subvert our system at its very core.

Blowing back at me along that corridor, a question started forming til it gathered to a roar: "How can you practice freedom law and not be free yourself?"

I shuddered at the implications of these words. They meant more than simply being free from fantasies about law, life,

and myself—more than being free to make my own
mistakes and learn from them.

They also meant I needed to unleash my fighter's will to win
where it would not unfairly yank the Blindfold Lady's arm.
Muscled with the power and prestige of government, my
warrior did that all too easily—bludgeoning all arguments
that blocked his way. Indeed, I seldom copped to it, but I
reveled in my power as a prosecutor.

Abruptly I recalled I'd chosen law to help the power-*less;* that
freedom law is fought for people *without* power; the
powerful don't need it.

Most of all I needed to be free from Machiavellian politics.
I had to be at liberty to pitch my passions without
countermanding signals from the dugout of expediency.

*Art, you can't deny the truth of these new revelations. But
like stepping stones across a foggy swamp, they seem
headed toward a single point. When you reach it will you
still be on the prosecution's side?*

I inhaled deeply, slowly letting out my breath. The response
was inescapable: Although honest lawyers can and must be
prosecutors, it won't work for me. The way I practice
freedom law can't now and then be held in thrall to politics.

This also means it's time I wake up from some pipe dreams
I've indulged in as a prosecutor: Dragging the corrupt and
powerful before juries of their peers; rising through the
ranks, forcing justice onto higher levels of authority; someday
maybe standing for election, extending freedom law beyond
the courthouse doors.

*Great Scot, isn't this enough for now? Abandoning these
castles in the sky is a lot to do in one post-trial afternoon.*

* * * * *

I steered my shaky Chevy home through rush-hour traffic,
dangerously distracted by new options dancing through my
brain. I indulged my old addiction to the contents of my
mind.

Should I resume defending indigents, minorities, protesters,
and others without power? Should I employ my courtroom
skills to teach law students clinically? Should I become a
processor of words behind a podium in academe?

A roadside plastic bag began to tumbleweed across my lane.
I swerved to keep its emptiness from threatening my soul.

Drusilla and I stayed up half the night discussing all these
insights and uncertainties. She wisely counseled me to let
things settle in the office and my mind before I steered my
life along another road.

* * * * *

Apparently I'd only caused a bureaucratic hiccup when I
freed the man my boss told me to leave alone; Clovis
Bankwood never censured me. However, I was handed only
routine office jobs, clearly less than courtroom plums. I
tasted no more misdemeanor trials.

It wasn't long before the sun awoke me with a whisper it
was time to make my move. To pursue my goal of freedom
law, to use what I had learned from practice as a prosecutor,
I must return to tugging on defense's end of rope.

With that resolve I drove our Yellow Bird along the parkway
from Virginia to D.C. By now the car's interior had been
chewed to tatters by our Irish Setter puppy, left one
afternoon with only setter thoughts inside a basement
parking lot.

I found a spot to park, walked to the office of my boss, and
knuckled on his open door. Motioning me to take a seat,
Bankwood seemed to be expecting me.

I thanked him for his trust, plus the first-rate education I'd
acquired as a member of his team. Leaving out the part he'd
played, I offered him my reasons for returning to defense's
side of court. He politely listened, disagreed with my
conclusion, but claimed to understand my point of view.

Strolling to my office—it was "temporary" after all—
I dropped personal belongings in my briefcase: framed
photo, stapler, tape-dispenser, two-hole punch.

Walking slowly from the room, I fished inside the pocket of
my jacket for the leather I.D. folder I had been so proud to
bear. I opened it to see my picture hailed once more as an
officer of justice for the United States.

I farewelled the secretary who'd first welcomed me, placed
the leather folder on her desk, and pushed through the self-
closing door.

AUTHOR BIOGRAPHY

Art Campbell was born in Brooklyn, raised in Appalachia, and scholarshipped to Harvard and Georgetown Universities. Prior to earning his second law degree he was a road-maintenance worker, janitor, boxer, rugby player, and professional musician. He became a trial lawyer for and against the government in Washington, D.C., where he also supervised students in the D.C. Law Students In Court program.

Campbell later moved to San Diego, became a tenured professor at California Western School of Law, and authored the country's definitive treatise on criminal sentencing. Married to the best-selling novelist Drusilla Campbell, they raised two sons and now enjoy large dogs and horses.

Breinigsville, PA USA
06 October 2010
246813BV00002B/2/P